Online Teaching and Learning for Teacher Educators

Online Teaching and Learning for Teacher Educators

Association of Teacher Educators Commission on Online Teaching and Learning

Edited by
Lori Fulton
Jon Yoshioka
Nancy P. Gallavan

ROWMAN & LITTLEFIELD
Lanham • Boulder • New York • London

Published by Rowman & Littlefield
An imprint of The Rowman & Littlefield Publishing Group, Inc.
4501 Forbes Boulevard, Suite 200, Lanham, Maryland 20706
www.rowman.com

6 Tinworth Street, London SE11 5AL, United Kingdom

Copyright © 2021 by Lori Fulton, Jon Yoshioka, and Nancy P. Gallavan

All rights reserved. No part of this book may be reproduced in any form or by any electronic or mechanical means, including information storage and retrieval systems, without written permission from the publisher, except by a reviewer who may quote passages in a review.

British Library Cataloguing in Publication Information Available

Library of Congress Cataloging-in-Publication Data

Names: Fulton, Lori, editor. | Yoshioka, Jon, 1963- editor. | Gallavan, Nancy P., 1954- editor. | Association of Teacher Educators Commission on Online Teaching and Learning.
Title: Online teaching and learning for teacher educators : Association of Teacher Educators Commission on Online Teaching and Learning / edited by Lori Fulton, Jon Yoshioka, Nancy P. Gallavan.
Description: Lanham : Rowman & Littlefield, [2021] | Includes bibliographical references. | Summary: "Written as a practical, easy to understand guide, this book is designed to support and empower teacher educators from all settings as they transition into and advance their knowledge, skills, and dispositions in online teaching and learning"—Provided by publisher.
Identifiers: LCCN 2020052096 (print) | LCCN 2020052097 (ebook) | ISBN 9781475861372 (cloth) | ISBN 9781475861389 (paperback) | ISBN 9781475861396 (epub)
Subjects: LCSH: Teachers—Training of—Computer-assisted instruction. | Teacher educators.
Classification: LCC LB1707 .O55 2021 (print) | LCC LB1707 (ebook) | DDC 370.71/1—dc23
LC record available at https://lccn.loc.gov/2020052096
LC ebook record available at https://lccn.loc.gov/2020052097

∞ ™ The paper used in this publication meets the minimum requirements of American National Standard for Information Sciences Permanence of Paper for Printed Library Materials, ANSI/NISO Z39.48-1992.

This book is dedicated to everyone who has taught or taken an online course, particularly those of us who have experienced and continue to experience the many challenges and changes in education due to the COVID-19 pandemic. Transitioning to online teaching and learning impacts everyone: K-12 students, their families, their teachers, and their school administrators as well as higher education students, their families, their instructors, and their institutional administrators. Together, we are a strong, dedicated and resilient community of educators committed to the social, emotional, and educational well-being of every one of us. Collectively we are yearning and learning to adapt to and advance with the ever-changing contexts of an interdependent global society. As members of the Association of Teacher Educators (ATE) Commission on Online Teaching and Learning, we reflect on the state of online education and the many modifications everyone is making, and we humbly offer our guidance, support, and care.

Contents

Foreword . . . ix
Shirley Lefever

Introduction . . . xiii
Nancy P. Gallavan

1 Inspiration, Aspiration, and Optimization . . . 1
Nancy P. Gallavan and LeAnn G. Putney

2 Global Awareness and Cultural Competence . . . 15
Marie Byrd and Glenda L. Black

3 Learning Content Online: Knowledge, Skills, and Dispositions . . . 31
Jon Yoshioka, Lori Fulton, Rosela C. Balinbin Santos, and Rayna R. H. Fujii

4 Pedagogical and Andragogical Considerations in Online Teacher Education . . . 43
Mark M. Diacopoulous and Brandon M. Butler

5 Authentic Assessment . . . 59
Amy E. Thompson and Nancy P. Gallavan

6 Meaningful Feedback in an Online Classroom . . . 75
Ashlie R. Jack and Shirley Lefever

7 Creating Collaborative Communities in Cyberspace . . . 83
Lori Fulton and Jon Yoshioka

8 Professional Ethics and Pedagogical Integrity . . . 93
Winnie Namatovu and Nancy P. Gallavan

9 Efficacy and Agency . . . 111
Walter S. Polka and Amanda Rudolph

10 Stories from the Field 123
Lori Fulton, Jon Yoshioka, John Hicks, Glenda L. Black, Rosela C. Balinbin Santos, Mark M. Diacopoulous, V. Carole Smith, and Erin O. Shaw

Epilogue: Challenges, Choices, Changes, and Cheers 137
Erin O. Shaw, Monica K. Amyett, and Nancy P. Gallavan

About the Editors and Contributors 151

Foreword

Shirley Lefever

During the pre-pandemic days of 2016–2017, when I was serving as the president of the Association of Teacher Educators (ATE), I chose the theme *Teacher Educators: Inspiring the Future, Honoring the Past* as a backdrop for addressing issues at the forefront of education. The intent was to focus on the positive rather than succumb to the negative narrative that permeated so much of the discourse surrounding education at the time.

By celebrating the profession, I sought to bring positive attention to teacher education, offering an invitation to the academy to shed light on the national teacher shortage and remind other people of the important role educators play in shaping our society. It was my desire to engage our membership in "telling our stories" and, through our collective voices, to begin encouraging more people to choose teaching as a career. I wanted to engage education leaders and advocates in conversations about effective support for public education, and to advocate for those people whose voices are not heard and whose educational needs are overlooked or not met in too many of the educational opportunities afforded to our students.

Nearly every one of us can recount an instance where a teacher made a positive impact on our lives. Telling these stories on a wide scale was intended to underscore the importance of a highly skilled teacher workforce and to emphasize the need for teachers who advocate for all of their students especially those students who are marginalized. The goal was also to shed light on the power of teachers to develop citizens who are literate, critical thinkers, knowledgeable, and serve as change agents and leaders in their career fields. This mission seemed particularly critical at that time given the social unrest and deep political divides in the country.

Sadly, the same issues educators were confronting during 2016–2017 are even more prominent today. The nationwide teacher shortage caused by a sharp decline in the number of high school graduates enrolling in teacher preparation programs has continued, with many teacher preparation programs seeing a decline in enrollment of 30 percent or more for each of the three years since then. This fact coupled with increasing numbers of veteran teachers leaving the field within ten years of entering their classrooms is continuing to contribute to a "greening" of the profession with growing numbers of classrooms being filled by teachers with fewer years of experience.

More importantly, the need to respond to the social unrest that was occurring all over the United States at that time is now increasingly urgent as the Black Lives Matter movement is raising the public's consciousness of the prevalence of the social injustices including police brutality that have been the fabric of our students' of color lives for far too long. These injustices are being made even more striking as data are being reported showing the numbers of black and brown persons impacted by the COVID-19 virus are alarmingly greater than other populations. The causes for this radical difference have been attributed to a history of systemic racism that has left so many of these Americans with limited resources to weather the prolonged impact of the pandemic.

In all too familiar headlines, in response to the COVID-19 virus, state governments issued mandates to close schools, necessitating teachers across the globe to turn to online learning platforms in an attempt to ensure learning for our K–12 students continued. Not surprisingly, it became apparent very quickly that access to schooling was a much more complicated process than simply sending out Zoom links to every student and teacher. Within a very short time period, teachers were faced with myriad challenges including learning new technologies, adapting curriculum to online delivery, and identifying strategies for connecting with students, families, and caregivers.

Income inequality and educational disparities that have existed throughout our history were amplified in this new environment as school systems across the United States began to grapple with the realities that significant percentages of their students were not accessing *any* educational resources. Again, the majority of students being left behind without access to schooling were our students of color. A large number of these students did not and do not have access to a computer or mobile device, and efforts to supply the hardware have been thwarted by limited internet access. All of these factors must be considered as we tackle the current challenge of providing equal access to education for all of our school aged learners.

The Association of Teacher Educators, as an organization, promotes the creation of commissions and taskforces among its membership to study specific educational trends and societal influences on current educational settings. As such, one of the commissions I enacted during my ATE presidency was the Commission for Online Teaching and Learning. The discussion in 2016–2017 regarding the need for such a commission was predominated by the growing popularity of online teaching for both teachers and learners and the need for informed approaches to online education. This book is an outgrowth of that commission's work.

While a great deal of literature exists on how to create online lessons for PreK–12 students, less information is available addressing the specific needs of teacher educators whose audiences include PreK–12 learners as well as both teacher candidates and classroom teachers. Whereas in 2016–2017, the interest in online teaching and learning was primarily attributed to the view that online teaching is more convenient and thus more appealing to teachers and learners, the concern today is necessity and access. Little did we know at the time that convenience would become the least of teachers' concerns a few short years later.

Now, in 2020, teachers and teacher educators are turning to online teaching out of necessity. Teachers everywhere are being forced into using this platform as a means of keeping students safe in the wake of a global pandemic. Now, more than ever before, teachers are looking for information on not only how to create online lessons, but also how to deliver online instruction in ways that build community among learners and addresses the social and emotional needs of learners across a wide span of ages and income levels. In this context, teachers and teacher educators must create learning opportunities that take into consideration hugely increasing disparities between those with access to resources, such as high-speed internet access, and those without these essential resources.

Returning to a message of hope and inspiration, as we look to online learning as a response to the need for a rapid solution to educational access for all students, we must remember who is at the heart of this change: teachers. We must also remember that our teachers are up for the challenge. This book is intended to support teachers and administrators who are in the midst of this change to ensure they have the knowledge to build on their abilities, their creativity, and their passion to create online learning environments that address the social, emotional, economic, and academic needs of their students. As it has accomplished for one hundred years, the Association of Teacher Educators, through the publication of this book, is staying true to its vision of promoting advocacy, equity, leadership, and professionalism for teacher educators in all settings and supporting quality education for all learners at all levels.

Introduction

Nancy P. Gallavan

Many concepts and practices accompanied by seemingly unlimited tools and techniques (e.g., Casey et al., 2018) are written about the ever-growing field of online teaching and learning. Likewise, myriad publications over time address the ever-expanding collection of established and developing theory, research, and pedagogy related to teacher education. However, few texts focus exclusively on online teaching and learning in teacher education written specifically for teacher educators. Our text fills this much-needed niche by enlightening, equipping, and empowering teacher educators to design and facilitate teaching and learning via ten dynamic topics.

We invite teacher educators to consider these ten topics in terms of the goals and purposes unifying their programs coupled with the objectives and outcomes distinguishing their courses. Ultimately, we intend for our text to guide and support teacher educators as they strive to advance learners' awareness, application, and appreciation germane to their teacher candidates' quests to become effective, career classroom teachers.

The ten topics presented in this text include:

1. Inspiration, Aspiration, and Optimization
2. Global Awareness and Cultural Competence
3. Content Knowledge, Skills, and Dispositions
4. Pedagogicaland Anadragogical Knowledge, Skills, and Dispositions
5. Authentic Assessment
6. Meaningful Feedback
7. Collaborative Learning Communities
8. Professional Ethics and Integrity
9. Efficacy and Agency
10. Perspectives of Students and Professors

As the authors' conversations continued, we began to identify Challenges, Choices, Changes, and Cheers we wanted to add as an epilogue. This epilogue became more important with the conversation to online teaching and learning due to the COVID-19 pandemic.

Opening with a captivating vignette, each chapter in this text examines the topic through pertinent issues from the perspectives of both the learner, i.e., teacher candidate, and the teacher, i.e., teacher educator. Each chapter features content that details critical descriptions, thorough explanations, clear justifications, and practical suggestions. Finally, each chapter closes with a summary connecting the chapter text with the opening vignette and overall topic of the text. Each chapter includes a list of related resources and poses reflective questions for dynamic conversations.

Co-authored by a collection of accomplished teacher educators who write from their individual and diverse expertise and experiences, this text offers insights and inspirations that will appeal to today's teacher educators who bring specialized academic knowledge and sundry technological proficiencies into their positions. This text recognizes the range of technological preparation and professional development attained by and available to teacher educators throughout their careers.

Some teacher educators were raised and educated in the digital age, have always accessed information and opportunities via the internet, and have automatically prepared a wide assortment of documents on a computer and other electronic devices. Conversely, some teacher educators have become acquainted with the internet, computer, and other electronic devices during their journeys as educators, both as learners and teachers. Notably, both groups continue to broaden their aptitudes concomitantly to increase their own knowledge, skills, and dispositions to modify and improve their online course design and facilitation. Mindfully, this text contributes to the continuing education that all teacher educators seek to renew their success and satisfaction; we hope you find it beneficial.

ONLINE TEACHING AND LEARNING

Preceded by distance learning when people engaged in teaching and learning via telephone and the postal service (Clark, 2013), online teaching and learning began as soon as computer word-processing and internet connectivity were available. The opportunity for people to communicate online provided both instructors and learners with boundless choices impacting their personal lives and their professional careers. However, early online teaching and learning classrooms tended to resemble face-to-face classrooms, rely on chat rooms and email (Adelstein & Barbour, 2017), and were not contextualized to the specific learners enrolled in the course—individually and as a group, in other words, acknowledging who they are, what they want, and what they are capable of becoming.

The process of online teaching and learning encapsulates well-accepted aspects of education that instructors want to make available and learners expect to be accessible. However, both instructors and learners envision high-quality teaching and learning experiences that build upon learners' prior knowledge, engage them meaningfully in their learning, create a rewarding community of inquiry, challenge learners with critical thinking and individualized outcomes, integrate content naturally with other course content, fit within their programs of study, and prepare learners appropriately for their futures, i.e., college, career, community, and civic life—futures that will be co-constructed by the future participants. Briefly, all educational classroom formats strive to establish a sense of place where everyone feels welcomed, wanted, safe, respected, and energized; has a sense of belonging.

These characteristics of high-quality teaching and learning apply to face-to-face as well as online teaching and learning and hybrid formats, yet each milieu is framed by distinctive parameters. In 2011, the International Association for K–12 Online Learning (iNACOL) published ten National Standards for Quality Online Teaching (version 2) (iNACOL, 2011). Albeit written broadly to encompass all aspects of design and facilitation (Adelstein & Barbour, 2017), the online teacher must:

1. Know the primary concepts and structures of effective online instruction and be able to create learning experiences to enable student success.
2. Understand and be able to use a range of technologies, both existing and emerging, that effectively support student learning and engagement in the online environment.
3. Plan, design, and incorporate strategies to encourage active learning, application, interaction, participation, and collaboration in the online environment.
4. Promote student success through clear expectations, prompt responses, and regular feedback.
5. Model, guide, and encourage legal, ethical, and safe behavior related to technology use.
6. Be cognizant of the diversity of student academic needs and incorporate accommodations into the online environment.
7. Demonstrate competencies in creating and implementing assessments in online learning environments in ways that ensure validity and reliability of the instruments and procedures.
8. Develop and deliver assessments, projects, and assignments that meet standards-based learning goals and assess learning progress by measuring student achievement of the learning goals.

9. Demonstrate competency in using data from assessments and other data sources to modify content and to guide student learning.
10. Interact in a professional, effective manner with colleagues, parents, and other members of the community to support students' success.
11. Arrange media and content to help students and instructors transfer knowledge most effectively in the online environment.

Each of these iNACOL standards (2011) is delineated into three to ten concepts categorized as Teacher Knowledge and Understanding aligned with approximately the same number of practices categorized as Teacher Abilities. We share the iNACOL standards as they readily apply to online teaching and learning in higher education.

Also, in 2011, Academic Partnerships published *A Guide to Quality in Online Learning* showcasing the Quality Matters Program Rubric Standards 2011–2013. The rubric identifies eight standards aligned with a range of four to eight items with assigned point values for self-assessment. The primary standards and secondary items are valid for criteria for teaching and learning in both K–12 and higher education. The authors of this guide promote ongoing policy review and professional development to maintain expectations by learners, teachers, and the institution.

In 2014, the National Education Association (NEA) published their *Guide to Teaching Online Courses* (National Education Association, 2014) in collaboration with the International Society for Technology in Education (ISTE), North American Council for Online Learning, the National Commission for Teaching and America's Future, and Virtual High Schools, Inc. This guide offers K–12 teachers with general strategies and specific skills related to online teaching and learning along with consideration of program evaluation, policy issues, and professional preparation of online instructors. Plus, the iNACOL Standards and NEA Guidelines furnish resources for teacher educators as they design and facilitate courses in teacher education, courses much different from face-to-face and/or hybrid courses (Hixon et al., 2011).

ONLINE TEACHING AND LEARNING FOR TEACHER EDUCATION

Effective online teaching and learning in teacher education involves the Five Spheres of Consideration of Teacher Education as shown in figure 0.1 at the center of a target, the Five Spheres of Consideration of Teacher Education is aimed on the engagement, connections, and achievement associated with K–12 learners. Consequently, our discussion counts down from number 5 to number 1 as the most vital sphere in the center.

Introduction xvii

Educational Institutions. The outermost sphere, number 5, consists of the education institutions and their individual teacher preparation programs. Teacher education can be found in high schools, K–12 school districts, community colleges, universities of all sizes and ratings, and private corporations; they consist of traditional and nontraditional programs. Every educational institution organizes and offers unique teacher preparation programs that may or may not be accredited by the Council for the Accreditation of Educator Preparation (CAEP) (CAEP, 2015) and/or ascribe to the Association of Teacher Educators (ATE) standards (ATE, 2010). Currently, neither CAEP nor ATE have published principles and standards specific to online teaching and learning; yet both CAEP and ATE advocate evidence of equity and excellence across all parts of every institutions' teacher preparation programs.

Teacher Educators. Moving inward, sphere number 4 entails the expectations of teacher educators. Again, every institution has established the various roles and responsibilities of their teacher preparation program faculty; yet, in general, most faculty are required to fulfill specific outcomes associated with institutionally defined teaching, scholarship, and service. Ideally,

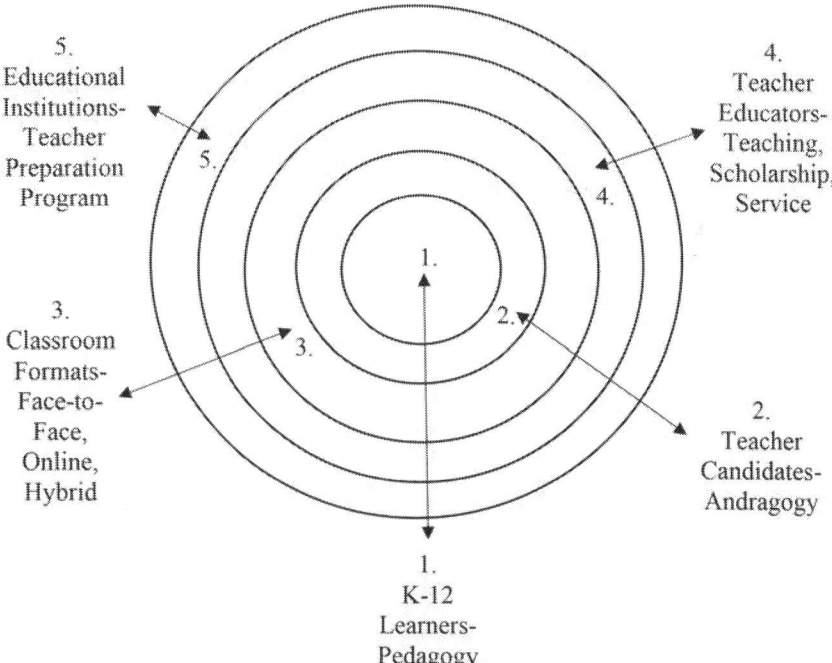

Figure 0.1. Five Spheres of Consideration of Teacher Education.

teacher educators advance their interests and expertise wherein their teaching, scholarship, and service inform and support one another productively with evidence of equity and excellence.

Classroom Formats. Sphere number 3 provides the space for teacher educators to determine the classroom format of their programs and courses. Currently, classroom formats include face-to-face, online, and hybrid (a combination or blend of face-to-face and online) teaching and learning experiences. Teacher educators must consider the advantages and disadvantages of online teaching and learning designed and facilitated deliberately for their teacher candidates (usually with regard for the institution's resources and faculty's capabilities).

Six popular advantages associated with online teaching and learning include: (a) flexibility with time, i.e., adding enrollment in an online course to a schedule that includes family, work, and other responsibilities, especially when the online course does not meet (asynchronous). In teacher preparation programs, online courses that meet online at given times (synchronous) tend to meet in the evenings respecting teacher candidates' day schedules given that many teacher candidates teach full time with provisional licenses or as substitute teachers; (b) flexibility with location, i.e, allowing learners to engage with the course content in order to complete and submit the activities, assignments, and assessments wherever they can access their electronic devices; (c) competency-based instruction, i.e, when course content and schedules are released early in the course, learners can pace themselves with the modules both meeting identified due dates and moving ahead when desired. Learners can adapt their home and work lives with their school lives to maintain balance.

Additionally, possible advantages of online courses include (d) potential savings cost, i.e., learners do not have to drive to campus, perhaps they do not have to pay for parking, eat in a restaurant, find childcare, and so on. With teacher education programs offering many online courses, some learners also save money by enrolling in more courses per term (given they have reduced driving and in class time) and earn their degrees sooner than originally anticipated; (e) an assortment of technological applications, i.e., online courses may involve a multitude of technological applications not used in face-to-face courses and/or electronically connecting with people around the world; and (f) a range of thinking and learning, i.e., effective online courses shift the balance of power from the teacher to the learner through the shared exchange involving every learner and the increased responsibility on the learner to read, review, write, and reflect independently.

In some face-to-face courses, learners do not contribute to the class discussions or interact with their peers. Online courses tend to require discussions submitted by every learner with comments exchanged with peers. The shift of balance is accomplished more effectively when content is communicated in ways that build on learners' prior knowledge and experiences, individualize the activities and assignments featuring creativity and practicality, various resources, and includes scoring rubrics that include self assessments and peer assessments when appropriate.

Four possible disadvantages of online courses address the requirement for rigorous self-discipline to manage the flexibility and responsibilities associated with (a) time, (b) location, (c) pacing, and (d) expectations. Learners benefit significantly when advisors and instructors provide guidance enabling learners to realistically predict the allocation of their time and energy and the accountability to their commitments; instructors are encouraged to organize their courses to help their learners gain confidence and competence via the shift of balance and of escalation of thinking.

Teacher Candidates. Sphere number 2 focuses on the teacher candidates, who are adult learners. Adult learning is associated with Knowles (1968, 1980, 1988), who published five pillars of understanding adult learners (Merriam, 2001). Adult learners possess (a) maturing self-concepts; they are becoming less dependent on other people and becoming more interdependent, self-driven, and autonomous contributing to their confidence; (b) expanding experiences; they have gained more education, read more literature, traveled more places, talked with more people, written more reflections, and have accessed more resources. Adult learners have acquired abilities to trust their intuition and tailor their intentions.

Knowles's (1968, 1980, 1988) pillars of understanding (Merriam, 2001) also state that adult learners possess (c) an increasing readiness and eagerness to learn across all roles and responsibilities at home, work, and so forth; (d) an immediate application of learning via critical thinking, decision-making, and problem-solving; and (e) an internal motivation to learn focusing more on consequences with rewards rather than consequences with penalties.

Acknowledgment of the pillars of adult learning enables teacher educators to capitalize teacher candidates' capacities—their maturation, experience, readiness, practicality, and motivation. Likewise, accommodation of the pillars can be easily accomplished by giving each teacher candidate a voice and choice in the course content and processes, opportunities to draw from their individual experiences to advance their learning, introduce issues contextualized in the candidates' anticipated professions, and shift learning to center on thinking and innovation rather than memorization and recitation.

K–12 Learners. At the center of the Five Spheres of Consideration of Teacher Education, sphere number 1 is the K–12 learner, the rationale for the four outer spheres. K–12 learners are enrolled in a range of school configurations. Teacher education strives to prepare educators so they may pursue their individual professional paths. To this end, teacher candidates enroll in a program of learning experiences involving two venues: institutional coursework and K–12 classroom field experiences. Appropriate for each venue, online teaching and learning aligns the anticipated knowledge, skills, and dispositions with the course purpose and identified content optimizing the concepts and practices of adult learning.

Essential throughout teaching and learning in teacher education is the understanding that three learners are present simultaneously: (a) the teacher educator, (b) the teacher candidate, and (c) the K–12 learner. The teacher educator teaches the teacher candidate through andragogy; simultaneously, the teacher educator teaches the teacher candidate to teach the K–12 learner through pedagogy, the teaching of and learning by children.

Understandably many pedagogical strategies are applicable to adult learners. For example, pedagogy emphasizes co-construction of new knowledge as learning in action. When and where appropriate, these joint activities certainly can and should occur with adult learners. Pedagogy emphasizes development of language across the curriculum. Language development is essential in every adult learning situation; however, the language or jargon usually is specific to the course content and practices. Pedagogy emphasizes meaning making by connecting content and practices to learners' past, present, and future learning and concomitantly their lives outside of school. Meaning making also is essential in every adult learning situation, yet frequently contextualized to specific outcomes and personalized by the teacher candidate for individual applications (CREDE & Teaching Tolerance, n.d.).

Both pedagogy and andragogy emphasize complex and critical thinking. Again, instructors of both adults and children must modify the activities and assignments so they are developmentally appropriate. Although K–12 learners tend to learn from pedagogy with more parameters, adult learners tend to learn from andragogy with more possibilities. Importantly, both pedagogy and andragogy emphasize interactive conversations.

PRESENCE, PERSONALIZATION, POSSIBILITIES

Online teaching and learning in higher education that is both successful and satisfying calls for learner-centered, teacher-facilitated, community interactive, action-oriented, time-conscientious, individually creative, and feedback-abundant (O'Malley, 2017) educational experiences comprised of presence, personalization, and possibilities. Instructors and learners must be fully attentive, individually connected, and comfortably open to new concepts and innovative practices.

PRESENCE

Garrison et al. (2000) define presence as co-constructing a Community of Inquiry (CoI) integrating social, cognitive, and teaching presence (Community of Inquiry, 2017) as shown in figure 0.2.

Social presence is defined as "The ability of participants in a community of inquiry to project themselves socially and emotionally as 'real' people (i.e., their full personality), through the medium of communication being used" (Garrison et al., 2000, p. 94). Cognitive presence is defined as the extent to which learners are able to construct and confirm meaning through sustained reflection and discourse in a critical community of inquiry. Teach-

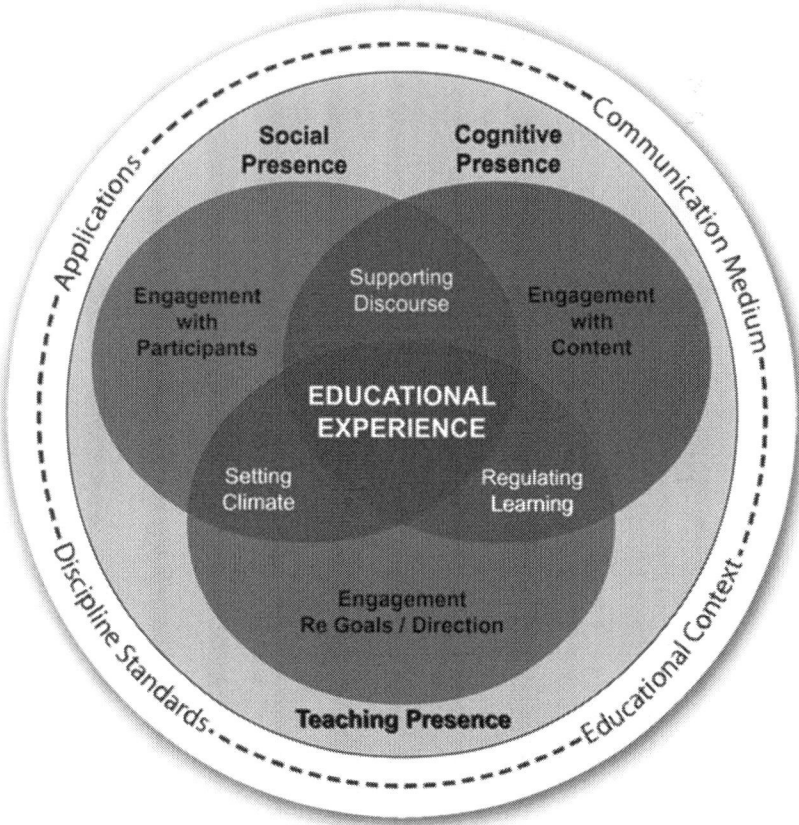

Figure 0.2. Community of Inquiry Framework (Garrison, 2017). *Retrieved from http://www.thecommunityofinquiry.org/coi. Permission was received from the authors to use this figure.*

ing presence consists of "the design of the educational experience," a responsibility of the teacher and the facilitation of the educational experience, a responsibility shared by teacher and participants.

Given the vast amount of content teacher educators want their learners to understand in preparation for their careers as classroom teachers, teacher educators must design their courses with clarity and intention. The depth of knowledge construction experienced by the learners relies on the teacher's ability to establish social, cognitive, and teaching presence (Shea & Bidjerano, 2009) mindful that online teaching and learning requires self-discipline, self-direction, and self-confidence. To achieve critical consciousness within each learner, teacher educators must optimize the information, access, and opportunities (Gallavan, in Wink & Putney, 2002) integrated through the course in ways unique to online teaching and learning (Gurley, 2018) that transform the learner from a teacher candidate to a classroom teacher.

Applying this Community of Inquiry framework, meaningful and worthwhile learning outcomes associated with each course in a program of study in teacher education must accentuate individual learner opportunities that optimize the social presence and the cognitive presence. To these ends, teacher educators must integrate five fundamentals across the online course structure, function, and direction much like using a map for traveling on a journey. The five fundamentals include (a) goals, (b) opportunities, (c) risk, (d) effort, and (e) self-assessment (Brown et al., 2010). In teacher education, goals not only demarcate the start and the end of the course, goals describe (i.e., answer "what"), explain (i.e., answer "how"), and justify (i.e., answer "why") clarifying the purpose of the goals and contextualizing the map for the course.

Opportunities allow learners to center themselves as the traveler and to choose their own educational experiences and/or the ways to express their educational experiences reflecting both social presence and cognitive presence. When learners express and exchange many different learning outcomes, the learning is significantly enriched offering more choices and voices for everyone to experience. The fundamental of risk when introduced with safety and reassurance invites learners to challenge and increase their current knowledge, skills, and dispositions with new and different possibilities perhaps unexplored in previous journeys. When the teacher and learners co-construct new understanding, higher order critical thinking occurs, stimulating problem solving and decision making leading to increased confidence and competence.

Personalization

A significant key to success in business is the personalization of the marketing and product. This approach also applies to online teaching and learning, especially in teacher education. Learners want teacher educators to use their names on email and feedback; likewise, they want teacher educators to set the tone and tenor on discussion boards where the teacher as well as other learners exchange observations and ideas. Replicating face-to-face classroom conversations and building a community of inquiry, via discussion boards, teacher educators model the power of presence and strengthen the sense of belonging (Rodriguez et al., 2019).

Learners also want meaningful activities that respect their intelligence and connect with their interests personally and professionally, allowing them to build upon their greater strengths. Most importantly, learners want feedback that clearly aligns the expectations with the outcomes and supportively provides individual guidance related to their social and cognitive presence. Moreover, learners benefit greatly when content and assignments explicitly identify applications for the teacher candidate (i.e., future classroom teacher) to use with K–12 learners (in that future classroom).

Concomitantly, much as teacher educators have long enjoyed their own customization in the design and facilitation of their face-to-face courses, teacher educators want to reflect their academic expertise and individual interests. Features and functions such as the web page appearance, content organization, linked resources, and, particularly, the teacher educator's communication styles, convey the teacher educator's dedication to the learners and the learning.

Possibilities

As teacher educators design and facilitate their online educational experiences, three categories offer seemingly unlimited possibilities contributing toward success and satisfaction of both the teacher and the learners. The first category, the learners, includes their expectations, readiness, identity (e.g., belonging), and participation (Kebritchi et al., 2017).

The second category, the content, includes the teacher's role in content development, integration of media, selection of instructional strategies, and development of meaningful, sequential content (Kebritchi et al., 2017). The third category, the teacher, includes the changing faculty roles (from face-to-face to online classroom formats), faculty motivation and support, learner-centeredness, faculty time management, communication control, and teaching styles, specifically interaction expectations (Kebritchi et al., 2017).

For teacher educators who are always teaching two spheres of consideration, in other words, the teacher candidates who are preparing to teach K–12 learners, the possibilities easily multiply. Raising teacher candidates' critical consciousness by providing developmentally appropriate information, access, and opportunities (Gallavan, in Wink & Putney, 2002) tailored to teacher candidates' future learners' cultural backgrounds, grade levels, academic disciplines, learning styles, and so forth enables the teacher educator to include links to inspiring readings and influential resources.

INVITATION

This introduction concludes with our invitation for you to continue reading our text specialized to *Online Teaching and Learning for Teacher Educators*. We have established a sense of place where you belong. The purpose of this book is threefold: (a) to mentor and strengthen teacher educators who were already engaged in online teaching and learning, (b) to guide and support teacher educators who were relatively new to online teaching and learning, and (c) to spark and reassure teacher educators considering the transition to online teaching and learning. As you advance the design and facilitation of your online course, we hope that the concepts and practices associated with presence, personalization, and possibilities resonate with you.

The presence of your online course indicates that you are ready for the learning and are receptive to every learner. The personalization of your online course shows that you are human and a caring individual offering your abilities to model and mentor via your expertise and experiences. The possibilities of your online course communicate that you, too (most likely) have been a teacher candidate and certainly a learner; you want your learners to be enlightened, equipped, and empowered as they prepare for their future classroom teaching careers; and you want the course to offer success and satisfaction to the learners and yourself.

REFERENCES

Academic Partnerships. (2011). *A guide to quality in online learning*. https://www.academicpartnerships.com/Resource/documents/A-Guide-to-Quality-in-Online-Learning.pdf.

Adelstein, D., & Barbour, M. K. (2017, May). Improving the K–12 online course design review process: Experts weigh in on iNACOL National Standards for Quality Online Courses. *The International Review of Research in Open and Distributed Learning*, *18*(3). http://www.irrodl.org/index.php/irrodl/article/view/2800/4176

Association of Teacher Educators. (2010). *Standards for Teacher Educators*. https://ate1.org/standards-for-teacher-educators.

Brown, J., Fenske, M., & Neporent, L. (2010). *The winner's brain: Eight strategies great minds use to achieve*. Harvard University and Da Capo Press.

Casey, M., Shaw, E., Whittingham, J., & Gallavan, N. P. (2018). *Online teaching: Tools and techniques to achieve success with learners*. Rowman & Littlefield.

Center for Research on Education, Diversity, and Excellence (CREDE) & Teaching Tolerance. (n.d.). Five standards of effective pedagogy. https://www.tolerance.org/professional-development/five-standards-of-effective-pedagogy.

Clark, T. (2013). The evolution of K–12 distance education and virtual schools. In M. G. Moore (Ed.), Handbook of distance education (3rd ed.) (pp. 555–573). Routledge.

Community of Inquiry (2017). *Community of Inquiry Framework*. http://www.thecommunityofinquiry.org/coi.

Council for the Accreditation of Educator Preparation (CAEP). (2015). *Principles and standards*. http://caepnet.org/standards/introduction.

Gallavan, N. P. (2002). Cultural competency for transformative education. In J. Wink & L. G. Putney, *A vision of Vygotsky* (pp. 157–175). Allyn and Bacon.

Garrison, D. R. (2017). *E-Learning in the 21st century: A community of inquiry framework for research and practice* (3rd ed.). Routledge/Taylor and Francis.

Garrison, D. R., Anderson, T., & Archer, W. (2000). Critical inquiry in a text-based environment: Computer conferencing in higher education. *The Internet and Higher Education, 2*(2–3), 87–105. doi:10.1016/S1096-7516(00)00016-6.

Gurley, L. E. (2018). Educators' preparation to teach, perceived teaching presence, and perceived teaching presence behaviors in blended and online learning environments. *Online Learning, 22*(2), 197–220. doi:10.24059/olj.v22i2.1255.

Hixon, E., Barczyk, C., Buckenmeyer, J., & Feldman, L. (2011). Mentoring university faculty to become high quality online educators: A program evaluation. Online Journal of Distance Learning Administration, 14 (4). http://www.westga.edu/~distance/ojdla/winter144/hixon_Barczyk_Buckenmeyer_feldman144.html.

International Association for K–12 Online Learning (iNACOL) (2011). *National standards for quality online teaching, version 2*. https://www.inacol.org/wp-content/uploads/2015/02/national-standards-for-quality-online-teaching-v2.pdf.

Kebritchi, M., Lipschuetz, A., & Santiague, L. (2017). Issues and challenges for teaching successful on line courses in higher education: A literature review. *Journal of Educational Technology Systems, 46*(1), 4–29. https://journals.sagepub.com/doi/full/10.1177/0047239516661713.

Knowles, M. S. (1968). Andragogy, not pedagogy. *Adult Leadership, 16*(10), 350–352, 386.

Knowles, M. (1980). *The modern practice of adult education: Andragogy versus pedagogy*. Englewood Cliffs, Prentice Hall.

Knowles, M. S. (1988). The modern practice of adult education: From pedagogy to andragogy (revised and updated). Cambridge Book Co.

Merriam, S. B. (2001). Andragogy and self-directed learning: Pillars of adult learning theory. *The new update on adult learning theory: New directions for adult and continuing education, 2001*(89), 3–14.

National Education Association (NEA) (2014). *Guide to teaching online courses*. http://www.nea.org/assets/docs/onlineteachguide.pdf.

O'Malley, S. (2017, July 12). Effecting teaching online. *Inside Higher Ed*. https://www.insidehighered.com/digital-learning/article/2017/07/12/7-guidelines-effective-teaching-online.

Rodriguez, A., Smith, M. D., & Magill, K. R. (2019). Critical humanism and online learning: Using discussion boards as a means of production. In J. Keengwe & K. Kungu (Eds.) *Handbook of research on cross-cultural online learning in higher education* (pp. 66–78). IGI Global. doi: 10.4018/978-1-5225-8286-1.ch004.

Shea, P., & Bidjerano, T. (2009). Community of inquiry as a theoretical framework to foster "epistemic engagement" and "cognitive presence" in online education. *Computers & Education, 52*(3), 543–553. doi:10.1016/j.compedu.2008.10.007.

Chapter One

Inspiration, Aspiration, and Optimization

Nancy P. Gallavan and LeAnn G. Putney

As a new assistant professor of teacher education, Grace and her department chair decided that Grace would teach two different courses during her first semester. One course would be taught as a hybrid course, i.e., face-to-face combined with an electronic format, and one course would be taught completely online asynchronously, i.e., an electronic format with no scheduled face-to-face or electronic class meetings. As a recent doctoral graduate, Grace brought experience to each of these instructional formats as a student but no experience as a teacher educator.

Each of Grace's assigned courses already had a basic yet functional online presence; however, Grace quickly realized that they needed much attention to meet the program's standards coupled with her own expectations. Before initiating any modifications, Grace viewed each of the courses through three lens: first through the lenses of the university student as a learner—every unique university student accepted into an educator preparation program as a teacher candidate; second through the lens of the K–12 student as a learner—every unique K–12 student for whom teacher candidates as future classroom teachers will impact socially–emotionally and cognitively; and third through the lens of herself as learner—the teacher educator establishing her unique professional career in higher education.

Grace labeled the lens of the university student learner as the inspiration or the goals and guidance she wanted the online course to offer. She labeled the lens of the K–12 learner as the aspiration or the objectives and outcomes she wanted the online course to promote. Then Grace labeled the lens of herself as learner as the optimization or the agent and accountant she wanted for the online courses to model. Concomitantly, Grace featured infor-

mation that would inspire engagement, access that would aspire connections, and opportunities that would optimize achievement. The unifying focus on information, access, and opportunities would empower Grace to establish the foundation for cultural competency (Gallavan, 2002, in Wink & Putney) *needed for the teacher candidates and teacher educator to collaboratively co-construct developmentally appropriate learning and successful outcomes for every K–12 student.*

Grace's experiences highlight three powerful overarching concepts that exist in every course: audience, approach, and self-assessment. This chapter explores these concepts and offers practical applications specific to online teaching and learning. Many teacher educators may not be aware of their multifaceted audience and the importance for tailoring their online courses to their audience. For teacher educators, the audiences are represented in a three-sided figure, as shown in figure 1.1: university students as teacher candidates, teacher candidates as classroom teachers teaching K–12 students, and the teacher educator. Too often, teacher education courses are aimed exclusively for teacher candidates without acknowledgment of the comprehensive audience.

The second concept, most likely, describes an innovative approach for teacher educators to consider before, during, and after teaching their online

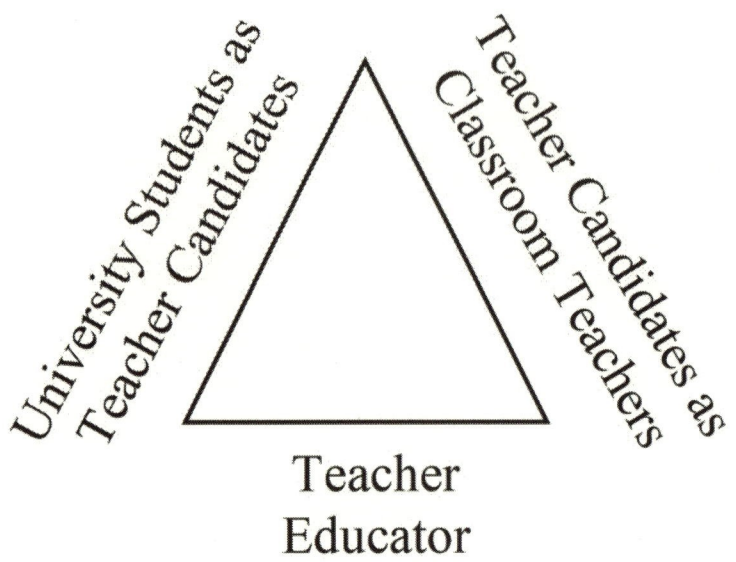

Figure 1.1. Audiences for Teacher Educators.

course. Approaches for Teaching and Learning, as shown in figure 1.2, contribute significantly to the continuous process aligning the preparation, facilitation, and reflection. The inspiration or *motivation*, aspiration or *outcome*, and optimization or *effectiveness* provide a balanced approach for teacher educators to apply associated with teaching, scholarship, service, and collegiality. This chapter discusses inspiration, aspiration, and optimization in detail.

The third concept, self-assessment, features three important words frequently used with teacher candidates, K–12 classroom teachers, and among university teacher educators: reflection, agency, and efficacy, as shown in figure 1.3. Reflection means awareness; it consists of a person's purposeful contemplation conducted holistically and honestly about the educator's thoughts, actions, and beliefs, usually associated within a particular contextual setting. Reflection involves an objective description of events, i.e., what events occurred; a realistic explanation of events, i.e., how events occurred; and a logical justification, i.e., why events occurred. Reflection also requires unbiased views from multiple perspectives. For teacher educators, multiple perspectives integrate (but are not limited to) the perceptions of university students as teacher candidates, teacher candidates as K–12 classroom teach-

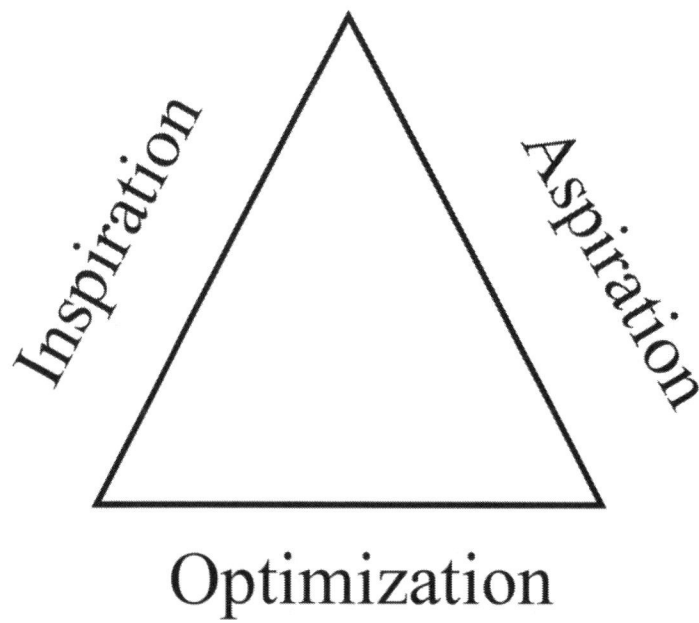

Figure 1.2. Approaches for Teaching and Learning.

ers, the teacher educator facilitating the course, teacher educators and administrators within the program, department, college. Teacher educators benefit by seeking feedback through various sources:

- Self-analysis and peer-analyses of recorded teaching segments
- Feedback (informal and/or formal) from observations conducted by trusted critical friends (colleagues)
- Feedback from students as teacher candidates
- Use of data collected from diagnostic assessments, preassessments, formative assessments, postassessments, and summative assessments that are criterion based and norm referenced
- Emphasis on data that are valid, reliable, and robust
- Self-assessment of evidence probing the description, explanation, and justification
- Journaling or blogging daily events, looking for patterns

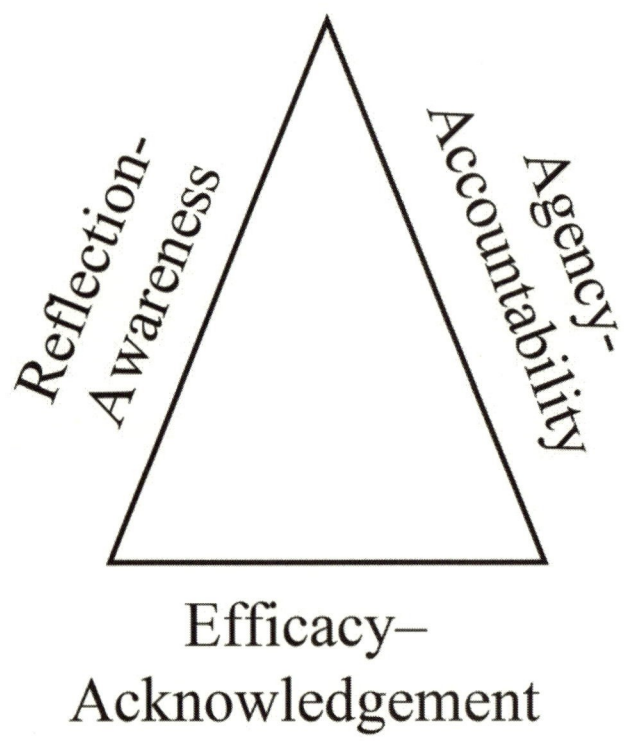

Figure 1.3. Self-Assessment for Teachers

- Identification of success, satisfaction, significance, and sustainability associated with positive and productive thoughts, actions, and beliefs

Agency means accountability of responsibility; it entails a person's capacity and ability to act with mindfulness and purpose with all people, at all times, and in all places. For teacher educators, agency consists of readiness to facilitate meaningful learning; receptiveness to candidates' expectations and contributions; and responsiveness to accommodate candidates' growth and course outcomes (Gallavan & Merritt, 2018) primarily through modifications to their teaching that guide, support, and celebrate learning.

The sense of agency for teacher educators is advanced when teacher educators interact in environments ensuring:

- Information
- Transparency
- Trust
- Shared Decision Making
- Engagement (i.e., goal setting, planning, preparation, assessment, analysis, change, etc.)
- Challenge
- Innovation
- Support
- Leadership Opportunities
- Professional Development

Efficacy means the acknowledgment of a person's ability to reach an outcome or achieve a goal. Efficacy encompasses confidence in a person's competence, allowing the person to offer understanding and acceptance as well as to advocate for change and well-being for other people and for themselves. For educators, efficacy offers a powerful construct (Tschannen-Moran & Hoy, 2001) for contextualizing and comprehending the range of compassion and commitment K–12 classrooms teachers and teacher educators commit to the teaching, learning, and schooling.

Bandura's (1977) four sources of efficacy include (a) vicarious observations, i.e., learning through the models displayed all around us; (b) social persuasion, i.e., learning through the messages we receive or we choose to hear; (c) physiological and emotional cues, i.e., learning through the mirrors we imitate and/or are taught directly and indirectly; and (d) mastery experiences, i.e., learning through the methods that we rehearse, receive feedback, and reap reward. Teacher educators facilitating online teaching and learning are encouraged to capitalize upon the four sources of efficacy both as concepts for their candidates to understand and use in their own K–12 teaching practices and as course procedures to increase candidate meaning, engagement, curiosity, connections, and achievement.

THREE CRITICAL QUESTIONS

As you read this chapter, delve into three critical questions that elicit valuable yet varied perceptions that readily transfer to and transform your personal growth, professional development, and pedagogical expertise. The principle of inspiration prompts the critical question of "Who am I?" The principle of aspiration probes, "What do I want?" And the principle of optimization provokes, "What am I capable of achieving?"

Teacher educators grapple with these three questions as they navigate challenges, choices, and changes that contribute to personal identification and professional reputation. Ideally, teacher educators not only want these aspects of professionalism to inform and support one another in their growing sense of self, but also teacher educators strive for these aspects of professionalism to be evident to their constituents, especially to teacher candidates enrolled in their courses, their colleagues, and their various communities.

Ideally, the three critical questions of "Who am I?," "What do I want?," and "What am I capable of achieving?" should be contextually integrated into every teacher education course to encourage teacher candidates to begin formulating their own personal identification and professional reputation.

INSPIRATION

Inspiration involves the "the action or power of moving the intellect or emotions; the act of influencing or suggesting opinions and outcomes" (Merriam-Webster, 2019b). Inspiration allows a person to brainstorm ideas and generate paths that will sustain the will to find the ways to achieve the identified goals resulting in an impact on the intended audience. Without inspiration, a person may not produce motivation and momentum.

Inspiration also is defined as "the drawing of air into the lungs" (Merriam-Webster, 2019b). Merely reading this definition reminds us to breathe. Frequently we forget to allow ourselves time to pause mindfully and think meaningfully about the anticipated processes associated with inspiration, perhaps even giving ourselves permission to consider new inspirations and to identify, or even pursue, different goals.

Thrash and Elliot (2003) share three important qualities about inspiration to consider when beginning new tasks: inspiration is (a) evoked spontaneously and without intention; (b) transcendent of our . . . self-serving concerns and limitations; and (c) required for the transmission, expression, and actualization of a new idea or vision. As teacher educators, we are constantly beginning new tasks with the discovery of new information, access, and opportunities for our teacher candidates, our teacher candidates' K–12 students, and ourselves.

Inspiration is sparked by things like listening to speeches, watching movies, reading biographies, witnessing struggles. We extend selected past messages and capitalize upon new meanings to move from the mundane to the magnificent (Klein et al., 2018). Making our discoveries visible contributes to the success and satisfaction given to and received from online teaching and learning. Relying on their professional education, experiences, and expertise, teacher educators allow their inspirations to generate an abundant array of developmentally appropriate content, activities, assignments, and assessments supported by links to innumerable resources.

Online teacher educators must stay inspired; we must figure out what motivates us, acknowledge our accomplishments, build upon our strengths, and visualize our next steps to achieve our *outcomes* with the greatest *effectiveness*. Inspiration alone is not sufficient, and we must remain open to receiving inspiration from multiple sources and broad perspectives to combine with aspirations and optimization as we transfer ideas into intentions into implications.

Grace was inspired to become her best self as a novice teacher educator embarking on her professional career and carving her unique niche in higher education. She was pleased with her courses and their possibilities; now she would allow for the spontaneity, transformation, and actualization of her inspirations to manifest as she prepared for her semester.

ASPIRATION

Aspiration is defined as both "a hope, ambition, or strong desire to achieve" and as "an object of such desire" (Merriam-Webster, 2019a). Whereas inspiration consists of the mental stimulation sparking the generation of the idea, and the motivation to move forward, aspiration consists of the sustained energy fueling the pursuit of the idea as an intention and hopefully resulting in desired outcomes. Inspiration not only precedes aspiration; inspiration is also recursive and continues to kindle new ideas and intentions that lead to impactful outcomes.

Setting reasonable aspirations allows for positive growth, confidence, and wellness that ignite self-motivation, self-direction, and self-reflection (Aulthouse et al., 2017). Maintaining a positive approach may be accompanied with recognizing strengths, expressing affirmative emotions, sustaining productive flow, expressing authentic gratitude, living a perceived calling, and experiencing feelings of hope, especially at work (Dik et al., 2014).

These definitions encapsulate Grace's intentions for her online courses. She wants constructive outcomes for her teacher candidates such as to achieve, stay positive, and breathe—both literally, to take in air, and figuratively, to give life to their teacher preparation. Together the literal and figurative definitions help lift the candidates and instructor. Specifically, Grace's aspirations for her online courses feature five overarching goals guiding her course design and development, as shown in figure 1.4:

- Enthusiastic engagement,
- authentic participation,
- significant comprehension,
- creative individualization, and
- pragmatic application.

OPTIMIZATION

Optimization is defined as the "act, process, or methodology of making something as fully perfect, functional, or effective as possible" (Merriam-Webster, 2019c). Human optimization consists of a positive awareness that reflects a motivational approach to the understanding of individual and societal behaviors (Ngu & Phan, 2016).

Figure 1.4.   Online Course Goals.

Ngu and Phan (2016) contend that optimization or effectiveness is complex, consisting of individual structures related to work productivity, physical self-care and well-being, values and appreciation, emotional self-care and well-being, and interactions with other people. As teacher educators consider their audiences and approaches coupled with criteria for optimization and effectiveness, they must be cognizant of their inspiration and aspiration attributing to the constant tension between realism and perfection.

All teacher educators must optimize their resources, judiciously focusing on the three audiences while balancing their inspiration and aspiration. Teacher educators acknowledge that all resources are limited, so self-regulation (integrating motivation, direction, and reflection) are ever-present. With online teaching and learning, especially with asynchronous online courses, teacher educators are both the agents of and accountable for time, energy, and reason.

In order for optimization and effectiveness to occur, online teacher educators may want to seek another teacher educator, a prior student, or a trusted friend to provide honest feedback as they design, develop, and deliver their course content. Unlike face-to-face courses that most teacher educators continue to construct throughout the term, online teacher educators can include a guest student or provide access for a peer to see the entire course contextually including all of the documents prepared in advance for the course.

Optimization links with well-being, a critical factor for teacher educators' success, satisfaction, and sustainability. Teacher educators of online teaching and learning courses must clearly communicate the expectations related to both the teacher candidates enrolled in the course and related to the teacher educator to ensure effectiveness throughout the course. Time, energy, and reason frame these vital conversations that must be communicated at the start of the course and may need to be revisited throughout the course both individually and collectively. Findings have shown when people establish, communicate, and adhere to their expectations, they and their audiences experience increased levels of happiness (Teshale & Lachman, 2016). Consequently, appropriate management of resources bolsters the online teacher educator's well-being.

With the guidance of mentors at her new university and from her experiences as an online graduate student, Grace will concentrate on time, energy, and reason as she selects the content, resources, activities, assignments, and assessments for her courses.

INSTITUTIONAL EXPECTATIONS

Most university faculty are not prepared to teach online, and many faculty have encountered varied, perhaps few, educational experiences with online teaching and learning. Fortunately, increasing numbers of institutions of higher education have created offices with mentors to provide guidance and support of teaching excellence contextualized for face-to-face, hybrid, and online courses. All teacher educators, especially teacher educators of online teaching and learning courses, are strongly encouraged to contact their university offices of teaching excellence and seek continuous professional development. The tools and techniques associated with online teaching and learning change frequently, and most likely the university has documented their expectations.

Likewise, much conversation is dedicated to the characteristics of effective instructors in higher education, especially in colleges and schools of education. Recognizing that most teacher educators bring backgrounds as K–12 classroom teachers and may be prepared to teach teachers, teacher educators may be acquainted with the characteristics of effective classroom teachers. However, the characteristics of effective instructors in higher education differ. Rather than interacting with children, instructors in higher education interact with adults of many ages and at many stages of their lives.

Characteristics of effective instructors in higher education (Meng & Onwuegbuzie, 2015; Saini et al., 2019; Slate et al., 2011) state that students want instructors who demonstrate ethics, expertise, organization, communication, and student-centeredness through their professionalism. Specifically, students want instructors who provide clarification of content and expectations, access to relevant documents and tools, varied teaching methods, summarization of information especially for assessments, motivation for participation, appropriate examples, new technology, helpful feedback, and individual sympathy and understanding.

Teacher educators want to contribute positively and productively to their teacher candidates' preparation; make a powerful difference for K–12 students when they interact with teacher candidates; and enjoy their profession and advance successfully, experiencing continuous growth and development. Teacher educators strive to become their best selves, fulfilling the characteristics of effective teachers while attempting to maintain boundaries with the online sense of availability to balance their well-being across their home, work, and play. Guided by the Approaches for Teachers, and following Grace's example of setting attainable goals for optimal online course outcomes, teacher educators can easily nurture their intentions to impact while achieving their expectations for becoming effective teacher educators of online teaching and learning.

SUMMARY

As Grace began her journey as a professional teacher educator in higher education responsible for two types of online courses, she embraced the influence of inspiration, aspiration, and optimization. Nurturing her five goals helped her maintain her own motivation to optimize attainable student outcomes and to ensure her own effectiveness as an online teacher educator.

As her first semester concluded, Grace asked her learners to post their belief statements about teaching, learning, and schooling. Joyfully, her teacher candidates shared many positive comments that reinforced Grace's commitment to helping each candidate articulate responses to the three critical questions ("Who am I?," What do I want?," and "What am I capable of achieving?") associated with the inspiration, aspiration, and optimization emphasized by the teacher educator. Grace listened carefully so she could facilitate an effective learning experience for everyone (Khattab, 2015).

REFLECTIONS

1. What is your inspiration as you design, facilitate, review, and improve your online courses?
2. What is your aspiration as you design, facilitate, review, and improve your online courses?
3. What is your optimization as you design, facilitate, review, and improve your online courses?
4. How do you ensure that you are fulfilling your responsibilities to your teacher education students as future classroom teachers via your online courses? Why is this outcome essential?
5. How do you ensure that you are fulfilling your responsibilities to your K–12 learners via your online courses? Why is this outcome essential?
6. How do you ensure that you are fulfilling your responsibilities to yourself as a teacher educator? Why is this outcome essential?

RESOURCES

Brown, P. C., Roediger, III, H. L., & McDaniel, M. A. (2014). *Make it stick: The science of success learning.* Belknap Press, Harvard University Press.

Carey, B. (2015). *How we learn: The surprising truth about when, where, and why it happens.* Random House.

Casey, M., Shaw, E., Whittingham, J., & Gallavan, N. P. (2018). *Online teaching: Tools and techniques to achieve success with learning.* Rowman & Littlefield.

Dirksen, J. (2015). *Design for how people learn: (Voices that matter)* (2nd ed.). New Riders, Pearson.

Forsyth, D. R. (2015). *College teaching: Practical insights from the science of teaching and learning.* American Psychological Association.

Goodman, S. R. (2018). *College success stories that inspire: Lessons from inside and outside the classroom*. Miniver Press.

Heick, T. (2019). Ten ways to be a more reflective teacher. https://www.teachthought.com/pedagogy/reflective-teacher-reflective-teaching/.

McGuire, S. Y., & McGuire, S. (2015). *Teaching students how to learn: Strategies you can incorporate into any course to improve student metacognition, study skills, and motivation.* Stylus Publishing.

Nilson, L. B. (2016). *Teaching at its best: A research-based resource for college instructors* (4th ed.). Jossey-Bass.

Richmond, A. S., Boysen, G. A., & Gurung, R. A. R. (2016). *An evidence-based guide to college and university teaching*. Routledge/Taylor & Francis.

Vai, M., & Sosulski, K. (2015). Essentials of online course design: Essentials of online learning (2nd ed.). Routledge/Taylor & Francis.

REFERENCES

Aulthouse, M., Kolbert, J. B., Bundick, M. J. & Crothers, L. M. (2017.) Positive psychology and career development. *Journal of School Counseling, 15*(15), 1–38.

Bandura, A. (1977). Self-efficacy: Toward a unifying theory of behavior change. *Psychological Review, 84*, 191–215.

Dik, B. J., Duffy, R. D., Allan, B. A., O'Donnell, M. B., Shim, Y., & Steger, M. F. (2014).Purpose and meaning in career development applications. *The Counseling Psychologist, 43*(4), 558–585.

Gallavan, N. P. (2002). Cultural competency for transformative education. In J. Wink & L. G. Putney, *A Vision of Vygotsky* (pp. 157–175). Allyn and Bacon.

Gallavan, N. P., & Merritt, J. P. (2018). Reinforcing MAT course goals during internship experiences via Gallavan's seven essential elements. In N. P. Gallavan & L. G. Putney (Eds.), *ATE Yearbook XXVI: Building upon inspirations and inspirations with hope, courage, and strength: Teacher educators' commitment to today's teachers and tomorrow's leaders* (pp. 43–62). Rowman & Littlefield.

Khattab, N. (2015). Students' aspirations, expectations, and school achievement: What really matters. *British Educational Research Journal, 41*(5), 731–748.

Klein, J. W., Case, T. I., & Fitness, J. (2018). Can the positive effectives of inspiration be extended to different domains? *Journal of Applied Social Psychology, 48*(1), 28–34.

Meng, L., & Onwuegbuzie, A. (2015). Chinese students' perceptions of characteristics of effective college teachers: A mixed analysis. *International Journal of Teaching and Learning in Higher Education, 27*(3), 330–339.

Merriam-Webster. (2019a). Definition of aspiration. https://www.merriam-webster.com/dictionary/aspiration.

Merriam-Webster. (2019b). Definition of inspiration. https://www.merriam-webster.com/dictionary/inspiration.

Merriam-Webster. (2019c). Definition of optimization. https://www.merriam-webster.com/dictionary/optimization.

Ngu, B. H., & Phan, H. (2016). Social and psychological adjustment from a positive perspective: Consideration of the concept of optimal achievement best. *International Journal of Learner Diversity and Identities, 23*(3), 1–11.

Saini, N. K., Sethi, G. K., & Chauhan, P. (2019). Assessing the student's perception on teacher's characteristics for effective teaching. *International Journal of Nursing Education, 11*(1), 90–95. https://www.researchgate.net/publication/330526248_Assessing_the_student's_perception_on_teacher's_characteristics_for_effective_teaching.

Slate, J. R., LaPrairie, K. N., Schulte, D. P., & Onwuegbuzie, A. J. (2011). Views of effective college faculty: A mixed analysis. *Assessment & Evaluation in Higher Education, 36*(3), 331–346.

Teshale, S. M., & Lachman, M. E. (2016). Managing daily happiness: The relationship between selection, optimization, and compensation strategies and well-being in adulthood. *Psychol Aging, 31*(7), 687–692. doi: 10.1037/pag0000132.

Thrash, T. M., & Elliot, A. J. (2003). Inspiration as a psychological construct. *Journal of Personality and Social Psychology, 84*(4), 871–889.

Tschannen-Moran, M., & Hoy, A. W. (2001). Teacher efficacy: Capturing an elusive construct. *Teaching and Teacher Education, 17*(7), 783–805.

Chapter Two

Global Awareness and Cultural Competence

Marie Byrd and Glenda L. Black

Jerrell, a White male from a middle-class background, is a recent doctoral graduate with ten years of public school teaching experience and four years as a school administrator in a suburban elementary school in the Midwestern United States. As a first-year assistant professor working in a teacher education program, he is keenly aware of the focus on his teaching in his annual evaluation. One of the courses assigned is a classroom management course taught 100 percent in an online environment. His experience as an adjunct instructor in teacher education was limited to a few face-to-face courses as a lecturer. The classroom management course will be his first experience in teaching 100 percent online. In preparing to teach his courses, where the value and appreciation of individual differences is of upmost importance, Jerrell realized he would need to know more about the teacher candidates. As a citizen in the twenty-first century, he is acutely aware that his teacher candidates will be graduating into a world that is increasingly diverse and interconnected.

> Diversity is inherently valuable. We are stronger as a nation when people of varied backgrounds, experiences, and perspectives work and learn together; diversity and inclusion breed innovation. Groups of more diverse problem solvers have been found to outperform groups of less diverse problem solvers and companies with more diversity in their leadership also tend to be top financial performers. (U.S. Dept. of Education, 2016)

According to the National Center for Education Statistics (2019), in 2024, the current minority population in public schools will constitute the majority. In stark contrast to the student population, current elementary and secondary teachers in public schools are overwhelmingly homogenous (82% White in public schools) with slight indication for future change (NCES, 2019). Teacher preparation programs preparing teacher candidates to teach in a diverse society will need to prepare their students to "help shape a shared future built on the well-being of individuals, communities and the planet" (OECD, 2018, p. 3). To navigate these uncertainties, the youth of 2030 will need to develop skills that value and appreciate the perspectives of other people and their various cultural characteristics. Further, students will need to have the skills to be agents of change in a diverse, globally interconnected and highly technological world.

GLOBAL AWARENESS

As Jerrell began learning about the teacher candidates taking his courses, he discovered that many of the students in the program were native born to the United States. However, some candidates were foreign-born U.S. citizens. As a result, Jerrell realized he would need to create and maintain an online learning environment that was safe, collaborative, and ensured that diverse perspectives were welcomed and respected. He asked himself, "How can I build a sense of belonging and respect the universal values of my students in an online environment?"

Although the literature has not reached consensus on the definition of global awareness, the common themes include: (a) respect for fellow humans; (b) respect of the diversity of race, gender, age, religion, size, and appearance; (c) appreciation for multiple and diverse perspectives; and (d) understanding of the many different ways cultural, environmental, social, economic, and political factors impact the world (AACU, n.d.; Braskamp et al., 2013; Hett, 1993; Levy et al., 2007). Teaching is a relational act and the ways that teachers perceive themselves as related to their students and the world community are central to being an effective teacher. Most people see their worldview as the primary overarching view and tend to interpret events in ways that are consistent with that view. According to Golay (2006, p. 7), "worldviews that are narrow, ethnocentric, or discriminatory run counter to attitudes conducive to teaching" in globally and culturally aware environments. "Shifts in worldview that makes it [the worldview] more inclusive, ethnorelative, and tolerant should be the goals . . . for education in general" (Golay, 2006, p. 7).

Teachers are encouraged to develop students' worldviews in a manner in which they see themselves as connected to the world community and feel a sense of responsibility for its members. This orientation is reflected in specific attitudes, beliefs, and behaviors including:

An appreciation of the diversity of the cultures of the world, and a belief that all have something of value to offer. There is also a belief that one's actions can make a difference. A globally-minded person thinks in terms of what is good for the global community and shares an awareness and appreciation of the interrelatedness of all peoples and nations. (Golay, 2006, p. 8)

CULTURAL COMPETENCE

Jerrell decided to consult with his mentor regarding teaching the classroom management course in an online environment. As the summer semester came to a close, his mentor invited him to join the final synchronous session of her online course as an observer and to take notes on any questions regarding the delivery of instruction. As Jerrell joined the course as a guest, the online platform allowed him to interact with the students. He discovered that in addition to the foreign-born U.S. citizens, a majority of the students in his mentor's course were females of a diverse race/ethnicity and/or culture. After the session ended, Jerrell discovered from his mentor that his online classroom management course would consist of the same students as they were specifically recruited for a cohort in effort to diversify the teacher preparation program. For the first time in his career, Jerrell realized that he would be the minority in the course.

Cultural competence involves the ability to understand, appreciate, and interact with people from cultures or belief systems different from one's own (DeAngelis, 2015). Byrd-Blake and Olivieri's (2014) definition of cultural competence provides insight into the complexity of the process through the various phases of development: (a) the ability to engage in self-reflection and self-critique of one's belief system about oneself, individuals, and groups of people; (b) the knowledge, understanding, acceptance, and appreciation of diversity among students (Ward & Ward, 2003); (c) the ability to demonstrate behaviors congruent with an understanding of differences among learners; and (d) the ability to effectively operate within different cultural contexts (NASP, 2003).

As indicated in the above definition of cultural competence, the initial phase of development involves the individual confronting personal misconceptions and biases surrounding diverse learners and learning styles (Gay, 2002). This self-reflective phase will allow for the educator to consider the social, cultural, and language backgrounds of students during planning and teaching (Darling-Hammond & Bransford, 2007) so that the curriculum reflects the full range of humanity that exists in students' diverse cultures (Ladson-Billings, 2000). Overall, effective teachers are able to demonstrate their cultural competence through their knowledge, skills, dispositions, and expressions about themselves and others through their words, actions, and interactions (Gallavan, 2010). See figure 2.1 for the authors Cultural Competence Development Process.

WHY TEACH GLOBAL AWARENESS AND CULTURAL COMPETENCE

The diversity of the teacher candidates in Jerrell's class reflected the diversity of the K–12 students the teacher candidates will be teaching in their future classrooms. To model and foster an inclusive, safe virtual learning environment, Jerrell recognized that he had to be responsive to the cultures, identities, and backgrounds of the teacher candidates.

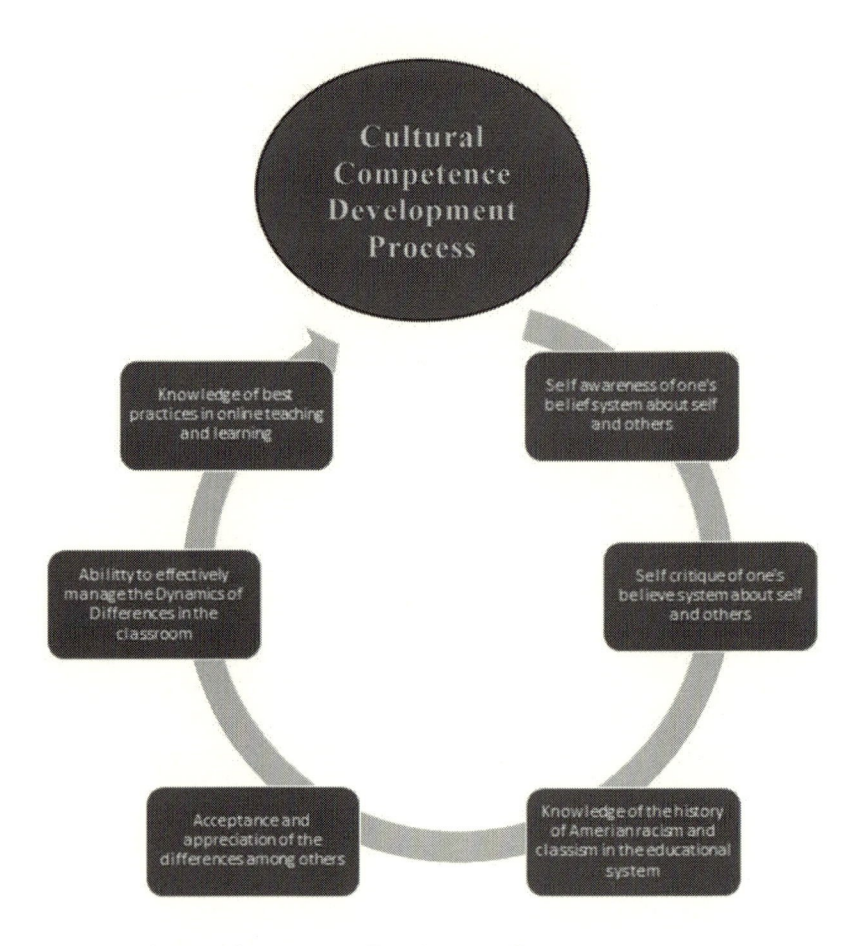

Figure 2.1. Cultural Competence Development Process.

To support all students in achieving their personal and professional goals in a globalized world, teacher candidates need to graduate from teacher education programs with the necessary twenty-first century competencies to ensure they provide educational equity for their future students. Fullan and Scott (2014) put forward a framework for twenty-first century deep learning competencies, known as the six Cs: character, citizenship, communication, critical thinking, collaboration, and creativity. Central to these six Cs are ethical values such as citizenship: "thinking like global citizens, considering global issues based on a deep understanding of diverse values with genuine interest in engaging with others to solve complex problems that impact human and environmental sustainability" (Fullan & Scott, 2014, p. 6).

Competencies related to students' identities as individuals and as members of their communities, society, and the world may be grouped into "personal and social competencies" (British Columbia Ministry of Education, 2013, p. 3), "civic literacy, global awareness, and cross-cultural skills" (Singapore Ministry of Education, 2010, para. 2), or "ethical citizenship" (Alberta Education, 2011, p. 8). Fullan and Langworthy (2014) describe citizenship as, "global knowledge, sensitivity to and respect for other cultures, [and] active involvement in addressing issues of human and environmental sustainability" (p. 22).

Building on the above competencies, the Center for Curriculum Redesign (CCR) (Bialik et al., 2015) developed a framework that identifies six essential character qualities for twenty-first-century learning: mindfulness, curiosity, courage, resilience, ethics, and leadership. Bialik et al. (2015) made the case for focusing on character qualities by suggesting that each teacher "facing the challenges of the 21st century requires a deliberate effort to cultivate students' personal growth and the ability to fulfill social and community responsibilities as global citizens" (p. 1). Scholars have pointed to the growing body of literature supporting non-academic, interpersonal competencies, which are related to strong relationships and long-term success (Duckworth et al., 2007; Dweck, 2010; Tough, 2012).

Jerrell reviewed the research on cultural competence. He also examined studies connecting the history of racism and classism in public schools to an ever-persistent academic achievement gap. His research revealed that the lack of teacher diversity, as compared to the student diversity in the schools, is considered as a component in the origin of the academic achievement gap (Byrd, 2020). To impact the academic achievement gap among underserved student populations, Jerrell realized that teacher preparation programs must focus on developing the cultural competence of future teachers. He decided to begin his personal growth with the first step in cultural competence development, a self-reflection of his conscious and unconscious biases.

Underserved student populations are defined as students of color from low socioeconomic environments, English language learners, students with disabilities, recent immigrants, and students who are the first in their families to attend college (Wolniak et al., 2016 as reported in Byrd, 2020). Culturally competent teachers embrace the differences among underserved student populations. Effective instruction involves the teacher's ability to address student differences within the essential instructional process so that the academic, social, and emotional needs of students are met and enriched.

The antiquated perception of a classroom being likened to a melting pot where student differences are molded into one cohesive existence does not recognize individual learning differences. A classroom with an effective culturally competent teacher is similar to a salad bowl where each item is placed into the salad and appreciated for its unique, individual flavor. Combined, all items enhance the overall flavor without losing its unique taste based on the individual ingredients. Cultural competence development is key for future teachers as additional ingredients are added to the salad bowl.

UNIQUE CHALLENGES OF EFFECTIVE GLOBAL AWARENESS AND CULTURAL COMPETENCE IN AN ONLINE ENVIRONMENT

Teaching Global Awareness

In developing his positive online learning environment, Jerrell needed to set the tone from the first day. He was explicit in communicating his expectations for a globally aware/inclusive classroom climate. For example, he clearly articulated (in the syllabus and in his online discussion) the norms for discussion that were built on respect and the opportunities to learn from each other. Jerrell acknowledged his position and identity and was mindful that language is culturally specific.

In the spirit of being openminded and with goodwill he gathered feedback using an anonymous survey early in the semester. He communicated with the teacher candidates what he could and could not do based on the feedback. Jerrell facilitated rapport building within the classroom by providing opportunities for group discussion. He also ensured differentiation of groups so teacher candidates would learn from multiple perspectives in the classroom throughout the term.

Teaching any group of students in elementary or secondary school classrooms involves teaching a diverse group of students accompanied with benefits and challenges. All students benefit from the multiple perspectives of a diverse group. Equitable interactions beginning in elementary and secondary school classrooms establish strong values that can last a lifetime. Nevertheless, students can create conflict in the classroom. For example, students in an elementary school classroom may make fun of or even bully a student based on perceptions associated with cleanliness, clothing, afterschool activities, or home. Students in a secondary school classroom may take a position against a student of Syrian ancestry when they are talking about their concerns of the Syrian refugees and the migration crisis in Europe.

Instructors on campus or in the classroom must be aware of their pedagogical actions. They are cautioned not to call on one student (or parent) to represent their cultural heritage as a whole to avoid creating misunderstandings. For instance, instructors should avoid asking the one Indigenous student in the class to speak for the experience of all Indigenous people in the United States. Indigenous students carry with them unique heritages, languages, and traditions, representing the diversity of Indigenous cultures (Black & Hachkowski, 2019).

Some students may come from the same cultural group and geographic region, but their differences may be due to community membership. Some students are deeply connected to their communities, and other students have varying engagement with their heritage. Other examples of a conflict may come from a heterosexual student calling out a student who may identify as lesbian, gay, bisexual, or transgender (LGBT). Similarly, White students may threaten Black students who present their views on affirmative action and other politically based issues.

Teaching Cultural Competence

Jerrell realized that celebrating the varying cultures of his students in an online environment would require the development of each student's social presence. He was perplexed as how to achieve this outcome since during the initial synchronous session of the course, the students were very silent and reluctant to contribute. Also, as students participated in the discussion forum, the comments were brief and lacked any personalization. Jerrell pondered whether developing each student's social presence was possible.

Developing and maintaining the social presence of each student in an online learning environment is a unique challenge of effective cultural competence. Many instructors are able to maintain the social presence of each student within a face-to-face learning environment due to teacher immediacy (Gunawardena & Zittle, 1997) but find the complexities of social presence development in an online learning environment overwhelming. Social presence is based on each individual's perception that the individual's presence within a group of people is recognized, valued, and respected (Al-dheleai & Tasir, 2019).

Whiteside (2015, p. 63) developed the Social Presence Model (see figure 2.2). The model provides guidance for people engaged in online teaching by identifying the behaviors related to social presence in an online environment:

1. Affective association of emotional connections among students and between the students and the instructor;
2. community cohesion through a culture of sharing resources and information among students within the group and supporting the success of others;
3. instructor involvement through instructor efforts to build a community among students by establishing relationships and making social connections;
4. intensity interaction of a high and consistent level of interaction among participants; and
5. knowledge and experience of the instructor in prior opportunities to teach in an online environment. (pp. 63–66)

The multifaceted components of social presence detailed in the model provides the needed guidance for instructors new to online teaching.

SELF-REFLECTIVE QUESTIONING

Jerrell reflected on his transition from teacher to a teacher of future teachers. Upon preparing for his online course, he realized the need to reexamine

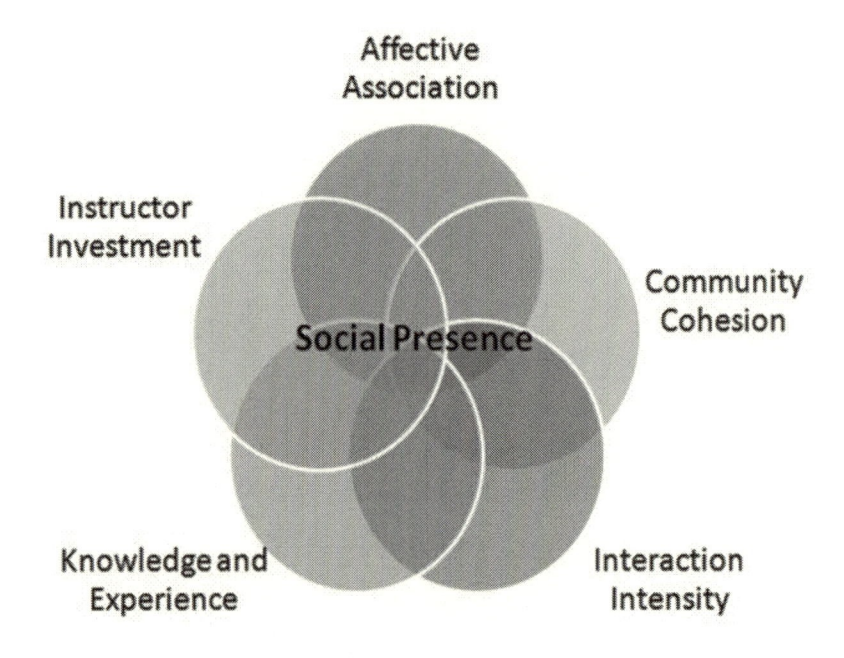

Figure 2.2. Social Presence Model.

his teaching philosophy and commenced to interrogate his pedagogy for the online learning environment. He asked himself, "How can I build a sense of belonging and respect universal values in an online environment?" Jerrell asked himself the questions to engage in the self-reflective process in developing an understanding of what it meant to be globally and culturally aware (see table 2.1).

BUILDING AN INCLUSIVE ONLINE COMMUNITY

Jerrell planned opportunities to get to know his students and for his students to know one another. To build rapport with the teacher candidates, he created a board/thread exclusively for non-content related discussion where he posted a short video introducing himself both personally and professionally. The teacher candidates were encouraged to do the same. In the video and in a written introduction to the course he shared how teacher candidates may meet with him. Considering the asynchronized nature of the majority of the course sessions, he did not schedule defined office hours; rather teacher candidates were encouraged to email Jerrell to arrange a time to chat on the phone or a video conference call.

Creating a welcoming and inclusive classroom allows all students to feel safe and comfortable expressing themselves and participating fully in class discussions. Specific guidelines for creating an inclusive classroom include

Table 2.1. Self-Reflective Questioning

Question	Global Awareness	Cultural Competence
1. How do I develop teacher candidates' social presence in an online learning environment?	✓	✓
2. How do I facilitate the development of a learning community of teacher candidates from varied backgrounds in an online learning environment?	✓	✓
3. How do I encourage teacher candidate self-reflection and sharing among peers of diverse backgrounds in an online learning environment?	✓	✓
4. How do I encourage productive work groups of teacher candidates from diverse backgrounds in an online learning environment?	✓	✓
5. How do I develop a learning community of local teacher candidates who embrace a worldview?	✓	✓
6. How do I develop the knowledge, skills, and understanding of teacher candidates to embrace culturally responsive teaching?	✓	✓

the following: (a) faculty and students have responsibility for creating and maintaining a safe and welcoming classroom; (b) ground rules should be established for treating everyone with respect and dignity by stating explicitly the norms for respectful dialogue; (c) learning is about expressing one's perspectives and listening to the perspectives of others; (d) learners are encouraged to be curious and ask questions for the purpose of understanding; (e) it is acceptable to agree to disagree; and (f) everyone is expected to share (the instructor's role is to ensure all voices are heard) and focus the discussion on the topic, not the individual (University of Denver, 2019).

Global Awareness Instructional Strategies

Jerrell knew that he had to explicitly teach the teacher candidates' global awareness. He facilitated their understanding of how important it was to respect and work with people from different cultures. To create a safe online teaching and learning environment, Jerrell began by clarifying the difference between debate and dialogue. For collaborative work, he mixed the groups to ensure all voices of the class were heard. In developing his classroom materials, he incorporated multicultural examples. Jerrell encouraged his teacher candidates to learn about other cultures to develop empathy and trust in other cultures.

To become more inclusive, it often helps to examine ideas through multiple perspectives. Gaining perspective begins with self-reflection, knowledge of regional history and culture, and service in the local community, but can be expanded globally. Studying abroad or volunteering for international service-learning opportunities are efficient ways for educators and teacher candidates to develop global and cultural awareness, adaptability, and self-awareness (Klein & Wikan, 2019). Allport's (1954) seminal work on intergroup contact purported global awareness and the reduction of prejudice involved not only contact but also the building of authentic relationships.

However, a trip abroad does not necessarily result in global awareness. Individuals may perceive themselves as knowledgeable or experts on a particular aspect of a culture without being able to communicate effectively with the community they are visiting. Rather, it is through entering the lives of others that we begin to enter their world, have something to compare ourselves to, and thereby develop a wider perspective (Brown & Hewstone, 2005; Wilson, 1982). Thus, globally aware teacher candidates need to develop not only knowledge of the other perspective, but also deeper personal understanding to "truly access the *appropriateness* of the behavior and communication" (Deardorff, 2009, p. xii, italics in original).

Collaborative Online International Learning opportunities have the potential to enhance teacher candidates' global awareness. For example, a nursing program in Minnesota and Iceland collaborated to develop an online international learning (COIL) project (Bragadóttir & Potter, 2019). The COIL experience facilitated global awareness for faculty and students by providing opportunities for future nurses to benefit from "insights, best practices, and collaborations with nurses across the globe" (Bragadóttir & Potter, 2019, p. 186). The project was built on an established university partnership. Critical to the COIL development were faculty from the two universities who met face-to-face to build relationships between the universities and nations. The following components were identified and determined in the planning phase of the COIL:

> (1) the objectives and extent of the project; (2) the content and the timing of the common assignments; (3) the website hosting the COIL; (4) the evaluation and grading of the common assignments; (5) the technology and grading of the common assignments; (6) the technology to be used; and (7) ways to evaluate the knowledge, growth, and partnership of the involved students and faculty. (Bragadóttir & Potter, 2019, p. 187)

Challenges to implementing the COIL included aligning web programs and time difference between countries for synchronous encounters. The first week students got to know each other by sharing personal information and posting video introductions. Students participated in weekly online discussion on a shared topic. The universities used the same assignment, instructions, and rubric, but each faculty assessed their own students.

Culturally Responsive Instructional Strategies

Jerrell remained a little perplexed as to whether his instructional strategies were effective, given the many student differences. In his effort to encourage student engagement and social presence, the climate of the course changed as students began to voice unaddressed issues related to equity in the posted discussions. The social and political facets of race, class, gender, and language tended to lead to disagreement and varying opinions. Jerrell decided to seek information on how to manage the differences of students in an online environment.

The key to effective instruction in diverse learning environments is the ability to manage the dynamics of difference. For an online course, effectively managing those differences involves a layer of added complexity. Student differences can also create challenges to effective teaching and learning. Instructors can manage the dynamics of difference in online classrooms through culturally responsive teaching.

> Culturally responsive teaching can be defined as using the cultural knowledge, prior experiences, frames of reference, and performance styles of ethnically diverse students to make learning encounters more relevant to and effective for

them. It teaches to and through the strengths of these students. It is culturally validating and affirming. (Gay, 2000, p. 29)

The culturally responsive effective teaching strategies identified by Ladson-Billings (1995) provide a solid foundation of how to appropriately teach culturally, racially, ethnically, linguistically, and socioeconomically diverse students. For online teaching and learning, those strategies will vary slightly due to the need for the instructor to develop teacher and student social presence remotely (see figure 2.3). However, communication of high expectations for all students remains constant in every learning environment. With online teaching and learning, this communication will occur via feedback to students on assignments, instructor videos, assignment descriptions, and announcements. Also of significance is the instructor's ability to encourage students to view content through their individual cultural perspectives. In an online course, the students have an active role in how the content is viewed and interpreted.

As Jerrell experienced the self-reflective process involving his views of those whose backgrounds and cultures differed from his own, he realized that he too held biases. He also realized that his biases were based on stereotypes he had never taken the time to personally challenge. Jerrell journaled his thoughts as he engaged in this process. He also decided to further educate himself on the history of racism and classism in the American educational system, particularly as it relates to student populations who are at the lower end of the achievement gap. Jerrell enlightened himself by researching global factors that impact education to enhance his ability to view other people through a global lens of how environmental, social, cultural, economic, and political factors impact other countries. With new understanding, he was prepared to effectively manage the dynamics of difference in his online classroom management course by implementing best practices in culturally responsive teaching and global awareness in an online environment.

Global awareness and cultural competence add a layer of complexity to effective online teaching and learning. Without the physical presence of students in the classroom, it is essential that faculty integrate best practices for delivery of instruction in an online environment with research-based strategies for instruction that enhances global awareness while sustaining culturally competent practices. The process of developing global awareness and cultural competence involves an individual transformation as change cannot be imposed by others. Rather, the individual realities must be independently experienced and developed.

During the close of the semester, Jerrell asked the teacher candidates in the classroom management online course to post a reflection on how they propose to (a) develop their personal global awareness and cultural competence and (b) develop their students' global and cultural awareness. Jerrell

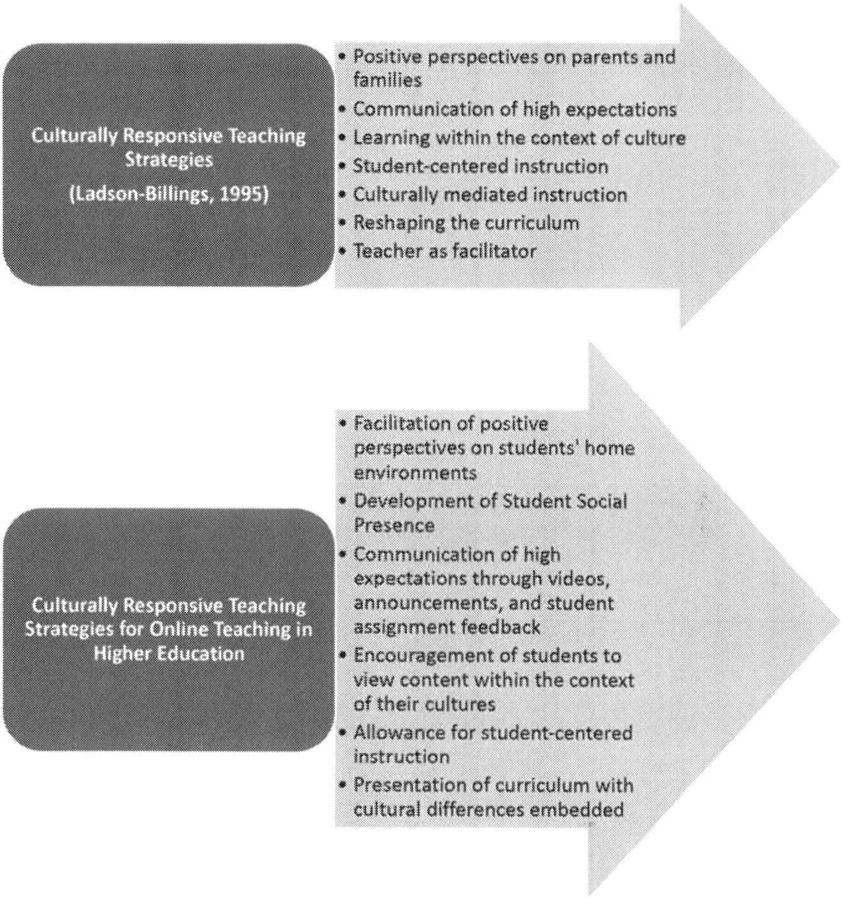

Culturally Responsive Teaching Strategies (Ladson-Billings, 1995)
- Positive perspectives on parents and families
- Communication of high expectations
- Learning within the context of culture
- Student-centered instruction
- Culturally mediated instruction
- Reshaping the curriculum
- Teacher as facilitator

Culturally Responsive Teaching Strategies for Online Teaching in Higher Education
- Facilitation of positive perspectives on students' home environments
- Development of Student Social Presence
- Communication of high expectations through videos, announcements, and student assignment feedback
- Encouragement of students to view content within the context of their cultures
- Allowance for student-centered instruction
- Presentation of curriculum with cultural differences embedded

Figure 2.3. Culturally Responsive Teaching Strategies.

hoped that a culminating exercise like this would build on the skills the students learned in his class and aid in the development of their competencies to become agents of change and to inspire their future students to value and appreciate the perspectives of others in a globally and culturally interconnected world.

REFLECTIVE QUESTIONS

1. How are global awareness and cultural competence connected?
2. What personal adjustments might you have to make when planning to develop teacher candidates' global awareness? Cultural competence?

3. What strategies will you integrate in your online instructional practice to enhance teacher candidates' global awareness? Cultural competence?
4. What should you anticipate to see and hear in an online classroom environment that will indicate you have developed your teacher candidates' global awareness? Cultural competence?
5. Of the elements you can influence, what might have the greatest effect to enhance global awareness and cultural competence?
6. How has this chapter about global awareness and cultural competence supported or disrupted your thinking?
7. What might your teacher candidates need to do to be best prepared for developing their students' global awareness and cultural competence?

RESOURCES

"How Diversity Makes Us Smarter." Katherine W. Phillips, *Scientific American:* https://www.scientificamerican.com/article/how-diversity-makes-us-smarter/

National Center for Cultural Competence; Georgetown University:https://nccc.georgetown.edu/

Teaching Diverse Learners: Culturally Responsive Teaching. The Education Alliance at Brown University:https://www.brown.edu/academics/education-alliance/teaching-diverse-learners/strategies-0/culturally-responsive-teaching-0

Teaching Tolerance: Being Culturally Responsive:https://www.tolerance.org/professional-development/being-culturally-responsive

The Center for Global Awareness:http://global-awareness.org/

Inclusive Teaching. The Derek Bok Center for Teaching and Learning, Harvard University:https://bokcenter.harvard.edu/inclusive-teaching

The Center for Global Education:http://globaled.us/educators.asp

World Learning: Education, Development, Exchange:https://www.worldlearning.org/programarea/global-education/

REFERENCES

Al-dheleai, Y., & Tasir, Z. (2019). Web 2.0 for fostering students' social presence in online learning-based interaction. *Journal of Technology and Science Education, 9*(1), 13–19.

Alberta Education. (2011). *Framework for student learning: Competencies for engaged thinkers and ethical citizens with an entrepreneurial spirit.* Edmonton, Alberta, CA. http://education.alberta.ca/media/6581166/ framework.pdf.

Allport, G. (1954). *The nature of prejudice.* Addison-Wesley.

Association of American Colleges and Universities (AACU). (n.d.). Global learning VALUE rubric. http://www.aacu.org/value/rubrics/globallearning.cfm.

Bialik, M., Bogan, M., Fadel, C., & Horvathova, M. (2015, February). *Character education for the 21st century: What should students learn?* Center for Curriculum Redesign. https://curriculumredesign.org/.

Black, G. L. & Hachkowski, C. (2019). Indigenous learners: What educators need to know. *Journal of Further and Higher Education, 43(8)*,1092 –1108. http://doi:10.1080/0309877X.2018.1450495.

Bragadóttir, H., & Potter, T. (2019). Educating nurse leaders to think globally with international collaborative learning. *Nordic Journal of Nursing Research, 39*(4), 186–190. DOI: 10.1177/2057158519856271.

Braskamp, L. A., Braskamp, D. C., & Engberg, M. E. (2013). Global perspective inventory (GPI): Its purpose, construction, potential uses, and psychometric characteristics. Chicago, IL: Global Perspective Institute. https://www.researchgate.net/publication/239931705_Global_Perspectives_Inventory_GPI_Its_Purpose_Construction_Potential_Uses_and_Psychometric_Characteristics.

British Columbia Ministry of Education. (2013). *Defining cross-curricular competencies: Transforming curriculum and assessment.* [Draft.]. www.bced.gov.bc.ca/irp/docs/def_xcurr_comps.pdf.

Brown, R., & Hewstone, M. (2005). An integrative theory of intergroup contact. *Advances in Experimental Social Psychology, 37*, 255–343.

Byrd, M. (2020). Capitalizing on differences: Keys to unlocking the academic achievement gap. *Multicultural Learning and Teaching* (published online ahead of print 20190003). DOI: 10.1515/mlt-2019-0003.

Byrd-Blake, M., & Olivieri, B. S. (2014). Measuring teacher cultural competence. *International Review of Social Sciences and Humanities, 8*(1), 55–67.

Darling-Hammond, L., & Bransford, J. (Eds.). (2007). *Preparing teachers for a changing world: What teachers should learn and be able to do.* Jossey-Bass.

DeAngelis, T. (2015). In search of cultural competence. *American Psychological Association, 46*(3), 64. https://www.apa.org/monitor/2015/03/cultural-competence.

Deardorff, D. K. (2009). Preface. In D. K. Deardorff, (Ed.), *The SAGE handbook of intercultural competence* (pp. xi–xiv). SAGE Publications, Inc.

Duckworth, A., Matthews, M. D., Kelly, D. R., & Peterson, C. (2007). Grit: Perseverance and passion for long-term goals. *Journal of Personality and Social Psychology, 92*(6), 1087–1101.

Dweck, C. S. (2010). Mind-sets and equitable education. *Principal Leadership, 10*(5), 26–29.

Fullan, M., & Langworthy, M. (2014). *A rich seam: How new pedagogies find deep learning.* Pearson.

Fullan, M., & Scott, G. (2014). *New pedagogies for deep learning whitepaper: Education PLUS.* Collaborative Impact SPC.

Gallavan, N. P. (2010). *Navigating cultural competence in grades K–5: A compass for teachers.* Corwin.

Gay, G. (2000). *Culturally responsive teaching: Theory, research, and practice.* Teachers College Press.

Gay, G. (2002). Preparing for culturally responsive teaching. *Journal of Teacher Education, 53*(2), 106–116.

Golay, P. (2006). The effects of study abroad on the development of global-mindedness among students enrolled international programs at Florida State University. Unpublished Dissertation. Florida State University, Florida State University (UMI #3232382).

Gunawardena, C. N., & Zittle, F. J. (1997). Social presence as a predictor of satisfaction within a computer-mediated conferencing environment. *American Journal of Distance Education, 11*(3), 8–26.

Hett, E. J. (1993). The development of an instrument to measure global-mindedness. Doctoral dissertation, University of San Diego, 1993). *Dissertation Abstracts International* (UMI No. 9408210).

Klein, J., & Wikan, G. (2019). Teacher education and international practice programmes: Reflections on transformative learning and global citizenship. *Teaching and Teacher Education, 79*, 93–100.

Ladson-Billings, G. (1995). But that's just good teaching! The case for culturally relevant pedagogy. *Theory into Practice, 34*(3), 159–165.

Ladson-Billings, G. (2000). Fighting for our lives: Preparing teachers to teach African American students. *Journal of Teacher Education, 51*(3), 206–214.

Levy, O., Beechler, S., Taylor, S., & Boyacigiller, N. A. (2007). What we talk about when we talk about global mindset: Managerial cognition in organizations, *Journal of International Business Studies, 38*(2), 231–258.

National Association of School Psychologists (NASP). (2003). *Cultural competence.* NASP.www.nasponline.org.

National Center for Education Statistics (NCES). (2019). Status and trends in the education of racial and ethnic groups.http://nces.ed.gov/pubsearch.

Organization for Economic Co-operation and Development (OECD). (2018). OECD Future of education and skills 2030. https://www.oecd.org/education/2030-project/.

Singapore Ministry of Education. (2010). *Framework for 21st century competencies and student outcomes.* https://www.moe.gov.sg/education/education-system/21st-century-competencies.

Tough, P. (2012). *How children succeed: Grit, curiosity, and the hidden power of character.* Houghton Mifflin Hardcourt.

University of Denver. (2019). Creating an inclusive classroom. Office of Teaching and Learning.https://otl.du.edu/plan-a-course/teaching-resources/creating-an-inclusive-classroom/.

U.S. Department of Education, Office of Planning, Evaluation and Policy Development, Policy and Program Studies Service, The State of Racial Diversity in the Educator Workforce, Washington, D.C. (2016).http://www2.ed.gov/rschstat/eval/highered/racial-diversity/state-racial-diversityworkforce.pdf.

Ward, M. J., & Ward, C. J. (2003). Promoting cross-cultural competence in pre-service teachers through second language use. *Education, 123*(3), 532–536.

Whiteside, A. L. (2015). Introducing the social presence model to explore online and blended learning experiences. *Online Learning, 19*(2). https://pdfs.semanticscholar.org/3799/52707fa658a503e3ed9c477d071a6502acdd.pdf.

Wilson, A. H. (1982). Cross-cultural experiential learning for teachers. *Theory into Practice, 21*(3), 184–192.

Wolniak, G., Flores, S., & Kemple, J. (2016). *How can we improve college success for underserved students? Through early, sustained, and multifaceted support.* Education Solutions Initiative, NYU Steinhardt.

Chapter Three

Learning Content Online

Knowledge, Skills, and Dispositions

Jon Yoshioka, Lori Fulton,
Rosela C. Balinbin Santos, and Rayna R. H. Fujii

One week into class, both Kai (the instructor) and Makana (the student) had the same reaction: "Wow. I really didn't expect this," yet through totally different lenses. Their stories unfold here.
Kai's Story
Kai was nervous. Preparing to teach any course, especially a content area methods course for the first time caused some anxiety, but realizing that this course needed to be taught solely asynchronously made life even more nerve-wracking. Kai had taught the course many times face-to-face and in hybrid sessions but never solely online. Student feedback indicated that they struggled with this content area, so in order to develop the best possible course, Kai consulted with colleagues who had experience successfully teaching online courses before creating new modules.

Kai wanted to create modules in which students would engage with the content, first as learners, and then as teachers considering how these learning experiences might translate to the face-to-face classroom and the online learning environment. As a result, in one module, students in Kai's class engaged in a hands-on learning activity by posting photos of the outcome of their activity in the discussion section. Then they participated in a discussion about how this activity helped them engage at a deeper level with the concept along with sharing a highlight and a struggle they encountered related to that concept.

Kai thoughtfully set up groups for the discussion to encourage richer dialogue; Kai assigned one student to serve as the moderator each week to synthesize the group's ideas and make explicit connections back to the content area methods they were learning. Kai felt confident that these types of discussions would promote engagement with the content as well as between students.

However, once the semester started, all of the thoughtful planning and instruction was lost to the fact that many students were new to online learning and did not know how to successfully navigate the online learning environment. With this realization, Kai adjusted the course schedule to include a module focused on becoming acquainted with skills for online learning to ensure that everyone would be proficient with the technology in order to engage fully with the content.

Makana's Story

Makana had heard from several friends that Kai was a great instructor—personable, knowledgeable, approachable, and friendly—and always willing to go out of the way to help students understand the content being taught. Makana was aware that Kai even remained a great resource and support for students after the class ended. Given that feedback, Makana eagerly signed up for Kai's online content area methods course with high hopes and eager expectations for what was to come. Then the course started.

Within the detailed syllabus were several engaging and informative hands-on activities, breakout sessions, discussion groups, and organized modules to help students learn and understand the course material. Unfortunately, there was also a serious problem; no one in the class really knew how to navigate the online class environment or how to use the tools Kai had provided. Makana debated what to do. Tell Kai? Or not?

After talking with other students in the class who were in the same situation, Makana was chosen by the class members to speak with Kai. Kai took it well and seemed already aware of the issue due to the significant lack of participation in the initial assignment. Changes were made, the most effective of which was a new module that focused on helping students learn the skills necessary to be successful in the online learning environment. The course turned out to be even better than what Makana had anticipated.

THE NATURE OF LEARNING CONTENT

Teacher educators seek to help teacher candidates:

a. understand the content for themselves,
b. apply the content to the classroom setting, and
c. consider how to engage PK–12 learners with the content.

Ultimately, though, all learning is dependent on the learner. Rothkopf (1970) asserts that all learning that takes place is largely dependent on the actions of the student, coining the word "mathemagenic," which means "behaviors that give birth to learning" (p. 325).

These behaviors are often social in nature (Vygotsky, 1978) and must extend beyond passive activities to build relationships and culture within the online community if content is to be learned. Furthermore, learners' interactions with the content must be meaningful and deep, engaging them in cognitive activities that require both lower and higher-level thinking (Dunlap et al., 2007).

This chapter addresses three main areas essential to developing these types of learner-content interactions in order to develop the content knowledge needed as a learner, teacher candidate, and future teacher. First, while content is often thought of as subject area learning (e.g., mathematics, science, social studies), in the online environment it is also important for the instructor to consider the content and skills needed to participate in the learning environment itself. Next, it is critical for the instructor to consider how application of and motivation for learning content influence the online environment. Finally, it is vital for the instructor to focus on the social aspect of the online learning environment and how community building and the development of relationships play vital roles in learner-content interactions.

GOT SKILLS?

Online learners must have online skills. This statement may seem inconsequential, but is it? Research indicates that the current millennial generation automatically comes with technological prowess (Papp & Matulich, 2011). However, instructors cannot assume that the students are prepared for success when engaging in online learning. After teaching multiple online courses, the authors of this chapter began to notice a trend. Students brought technological experience and exposure, yet students demonstrated only intermittent proficiency in academic online learning skills and systems.

While students may be accustomed to using technology, they may not be familiar with the classroom tools or technological platforms necessary for online learning. As Kai discovered when Makana shared their class's concerns, before instructors can get started on the content, they need to assess the students' proficiency in online skills and strategies for the virtual classroom.

Setting Aside Time

Instructors often consider content, pedagogy, and timing with the assumption that students who have elected to take an online course already possess the necessary technological skills and online strategies. However, in practice, this assumption may not be the case, and setting time aside to address the technological skills the students need to be successful in the class has been found to be essential. Student knowledge varies widely and their ranges of experiences affect course content and structure. Table 3.1 offers suggestions to create safe spaces for students to learn the necessary skills and strategies.

Delivery Matters

Instructors should consider the delivery of their courses. What frameworks might be influencing their choice of delivery? How does the type of delivery interact with the online skills and strategies that students might bring with them?

Delivery greatly impacts both actual and perceived student and instructor success. For example, if an asynchronous course provided content information, then required a product based on that content (intentionally leaving out community/peer interaction), online strategies would center on skills in acquiring and submitting information. However, if a course were delivered in a blended fashion, applying synchronous or asynchronous methods of instruction (Picciano, 2018), students may also be required to engage in a virtual community with their peers.

Though a subtle difference, the social, cognitive, and teaching presence as described by the Community of Inquiry framework (Swan et al., 2009) could be significantly impacted. The blended delivery system requires more skills of the student but results in more favorable outcomes in regard to presence. Table 3.2 provides examples of how delivery systems may significantly affect the necessary tools and skills an online learner may need to be proficient.

Table 3.1. Suggestions to Create a Space for Students to Learn Necessary Skills and Strategies

During Instructional Time	Outside of Instructional Time
• Survey students early during course anonymously to gather information on their experiences with course's online systems. • Build in time for questions (as questions arise or front loaded with anticipated issues). • Invite a technology specialist/instructor to walk students through various systems. • Provide mid-point check-ins for students to share their ability to navigate the course.	• Create asynchronous videos (e.g., screencastify add-on) to take students step by step through course requirements, etc. • Conduct office hours or conferences with focused topics to support students' online learning needs

Makana's feedback regarding the class's inability to navigate the online course confirmed Kai's inclination to modify his instruction. By establishing a safe sense of place and equipping the students with online technology and learning strategies, Kai modeled good teaching practices which helped his students transition from a face-to-face to an online environment. However, good teaching practices are not the only thing that will help instructors or students experience success.

ARE YOU MOTIVATED TO SUCCEED?

What factors motivate someone to start and finish an online course? Why are some students more likely to succeed in an online environment than other students? As educators, one of the most important aspects of teaching and learning to consider is whether or not what is taught is actually being learned. Many factors contribute to whether or not concepts, skills, and dispositions

Table 3.2. Online Delivery Systems—Tools and Skills Needed for Instructors and Students to Be Proficient

Online asynchronous only (no peer interaction)	Blended Online synchronous and asynchronous sessions	Combination of physical face-to-face and online asynchronous	Combination of physical face-to-face, online synchronous, and asynchronous
• course calendar • student resources and information • submission system	• course calendar • online community posts • student resources and information • submission system • synchronous virtual classroom engagement and navigation	• course calendar • knowledge of digital citizenship during physical face-to-face sessions • online community posts • presentation skills for physical face-to-face sessions • student resources and information • submission system	• course calendar • knowledge of digital citizenship during physical face-to-face sessions • online community posts • presentation skills for physical face-to-face sessions • student resources and information • submission system • synchronous virtual classroom engagement, and navigation

being taught are learned with one of the most important factors centered on the motivation of the individual.

The answer to these and other questions can be found by looking at teaching and learning through the lens of the Expectancy-Value Theory of Motivation (Wigfield & Eccles, 2000). This theory focuses on the belief that "individuals' choice, persistence, and performance can be explained by their beliefs about how well they will do on the activity and the extent to which they value the activity" (Wigfield & Eccles, 2000, p. 68).

When developing content for an online course, it is essential for instructors to consider choice, persistence, and performance as well as to look at the utility value and cost of the activity. In education, utility value refers to how useful an activity is determined to be with respect to an individual student's future plans (e.g., taking a course to fulfill a degree, or completing a degree to obtain a certain job); cost refers to how taking part in an activity might "cost" a student by limiting their access to other activities or entailing some additional type of (e.g., emotional, physical, etc.) cost to pursue their plans.

Vanslambrouck et al. (2019) advanced the idea of Expectancy-Value a step further by focusing on what factors affect online self-regulated learning (SRL) behaviors for students in blended learning environments. For someone like Makana, who exhibited a high level of self-regulated learning behavior, it was natural that if a potential problem arose, to actively seek out a win-win solution.

Once it became clear that there was an issue with using the technology required for the course, the first step for the students was to reflect on the solution, and the second step was to determine if the issue was personal or more widespread. The final step was for the students to decide to let the instructor know of the students' concerns and helping work through potential solutions. Students who exhibit a lower level of self-regulated behavior would likely require more guidance than Makana needed in working toward a mutually beneficial solution or would need support from an instructor or peer to actively help them with finding a solution.

Taking into consideration SRL behaviors, instructors can construct courses to support students with different needs (i.e., high, moderate, or low SRL profiles). For example, Vanslambrouck et al. (2019) suggested that high SRL students may, in general, require less support, but these students could be offered opportunities to collaborate more with their peers that should benefit both them and students with low or moderate SRL profiles. Suggestions for instructors include creating environments that include more group work or acting as a visible role model who effectively uses the online environment to share information and bring other students together.

For students with low SRL profiles, Vanslambrouck et al. (2019) suggested that learning more effective time management and self-evaluation strategies could be helpful. Instructor supports for these strategies could include working with (teaching) the students to use online planning tools and helping students to use online feedback and self-evaluation prompts. Vanslambrouck et al. also emphasized that, "teachers should demonstrate the use and personal value of their education to students" (p. 134). Toward this end, Vanslambrouck et al. suggested getting to know the students so authentic tasks and relevant examples can be integrated into the course. Building, cultivating, and maintaining these relationships encompass three essential facets that contribute to creating a free flowing, mutually beneficial, online learning community.

Kai understood the busy lives that students lead and worked hard to incorporate aspects into the course that would motivate students to engage with the content to help ensure that learning took place. This goal included making direct connections to the field whenever possible so students could see the relevancy of the work students were producing, incorporating strategies to support self-regulated learning, and developing authentic tasks to build intrinsic interest, and, most noteworthy, getting to know the students. This student-centered focus, validated by conversations with trusted peers, was important to Makana as were the many benefits Kai's course could offer. Knowing these qualities, Makana signed up for the course with high expectations of what was to come.

WHY COMMUNITY?

As educators, it is important to create unique and innovative ways to build community within courses and to forge positive, mutually beneficial, rich, and rewarding relationships with students. While many instructors are familiar with how to accomplish this outcome in face-to-face situations, this experience does not always occur naturally in the online environment. The challenge becomes how to create an environment where both the instructor and students gain a sense of connectedness (Swan et al., 2009) as they might if they were physically together. The ultimate goal for students is to feel a sense of belonging within a community of online learners while simultaneously achieving the expected course content knowledge, skills, and dispositions.

Community can be defined in multiple ways and across disciplines, including education. One common element is that community is about people who have a shared purpose and interest. Palloff and Pratt (2004) previously identified six elements of community: (a) people, (b) shared purpose, (c) guidelines, (d) technology, (e) collaborative learning, and (f) reflective practice. Since their original publication, they have added (g) social presence as a seventh critical element of the online community and collaborative work. Social presence is defined as a feeling of community and connection among learners that positively contributes to learning outcomes and learner satisfaction with online courses (Palloff & Pratt, 2005).

Instructors should want students to be able to experience the online learning community as a safe, positive learning environment where they feel valued and respected (Ritter & Polnick, 2008). Providing students with varied opportunities to actively engage and fully participate in their learning experiences is essential. Vesely et al. (2007) found that "instructors play a key role in motivating students to engage as learning community members" (p. 236). Instructors need to be aware of this effective teaching strategy and establish community early in the course to facilitate meaningful learning experiences.

Creating opportunities for students to engage in collaborative discussions and interactive experiences requires a skill set that may take time to learn and grasp. It is the instructor's responsibility to embed these initial learning opportunities into the course structure and curriculum. For example, this outcome occurred when Kai included an online module to support students in navigating the tools for online learning in the course.

Toward this end, there are four phases to creating collaboration within an online community: (a) Create the Environment, (b) Model the Process, (c) Guide the Process, and (d) Evaluate the Process (Palloff & Pratt, 2004). It is important to note that the responsibility of the instructor to support collaboration does not end after modeling the process, rather supporting students becomes even more significant for the instructor to guide, evaluate, and continue to be actively involved in the online learning community.

Creating an intellectually safe, respectful environment is essential, and once students have become comfortable with the technical skills needed to succeed in the course, instructors need to continue to model and guide the process to ensure that students are responding to one another in a respectful and constructive manner. These expectations comprise an ongoing process. Instructors cannot assume that just because the system was created that it will continue to function perfectly; systems, interactions, and behaviors must be constantly monitored, guided, and evaluated in order to ensure that the classroom environment is a safe, mutually respectful online community.

Creating community in an online course requires time, patience, flexibility, and recognition that the process most likely will be accompanied with both challenges and opportunities for both the instructor and the students. The instructor plays many roles including curriculum developer, motivator, and creator of a collaborative space. Of the four factors that Vesely et al. (2007) found relevant to building community:

- instructor modeling,
- student's interest and priority for the course,
- sufficient time for discussion and interaction, and

- interaction and dialogue

Students found that instructor modeling was the most important while, interestingly, it was least important for faculty.

When instructors possess an openness to modeling new and innovative ways to engage students in online learning and using a variety of multimedia resources, as instructors might demonstrate in actual face-to-face courses, the reward of creating an online community of learners can be transformative. Even though this class was Kai's first time teaching an online course, the experience created a new platform through which to teach and deliver content, and along with it, the opportunity for the creative, imaginative transformation of active learning experiences created specifically for developing community.

Knowing that the instructor plays a vital role in the online course, Kai tried to implement innovative projects that motivated the students, created a sense of investment in the online community, and promoted flow (Rodríguez-Ardura & Meseguer-Artola, 2018). In an online course, "flow" occurs when an activity peaks student engagement and time seems to pass quickly. The process was extremely challenging, but Kai never wavered due to feeling anxious or unsure about how to effectively create the desired learning community.

Teaching online has evolved from simply assigning students independent assignments to complete with minimal to no teacher-student or student-teacher interactions or peer-to-peer collaboration into the active presence and involvement of the instructor and students throughout the online course. Kai's and Makana's stories serve as reminders of how essential it is for the instructor to be present, to be actively engaged, and to play a key role in facilitating online learning experiences for all students. Dedication to effective online student-centered community building motivates students to acquire content knowledge, skills, and dispositions while simultaneously creating a positive, cohesive community of learners.

SUMMARY

Kai and Makana collaborated on a successful online learning experience that led to the development of content knowledge, skills, and dispositions that benefited the students as both learners in the course as well as adding to their toolkit as future teachers in their own classrooms. The success of this course was dependent on many aspects including the community Kai helped establish that allowed the students to feel safe enough to come forward and share their thoughts when difficulties arose.

While Kai's ultimate goal was to ensure that students learned content area methods, Kai also recognized that content alone would not be learned if students did not have the skills needed to navigate the course tools, the motivation to participate and persist in the course if difficulties arose, and a sense of community that allowed them to take risks and be vulnerable with one another. Good instructors like Kai can help students understand and apply the content in their classrooms to engage PK–12 learners, but effective instructors also often learn as much from their students as their students learn from them. Being open, available, and flexible are three characteristics that benefit not only the student, but also the instructor, in any online, hybrid, or face-to-face learning environment.

REFLECTION QUESTIONS

1. Considering your beliefs and preferences for online delivery, how do your ideas influence the way you structure your course? How does this influence student development of community, content knowledge, skills, and dispositions?
2. What motivates your students? And how can you use this information to better help them succeed in learning the content of your online course?
3. What skills do your students need to know and understand before they can learn the content associated with your course?
4. How do you create opportunities for students to build community in an online learning environment?

RESOURCES

Readings:
Cook, J. P., & Palmer, R. J. (2018). Learning to integrate digital technologies and pedagogical innovations: An exploratory investigation. *Ubiquitous Learning: An International Journal*, *10*(4), 25–37.
Picciano, A. G. (2018). *Online education: foundations, planning, and pedagogy*. Routledge.

Tools for Presenting Content Information:
Google Slides. The online chrome version of PowerPoint.
Buncee. Kid-friendly PowerPoint-style presentations. Allows for access to image searches, without searching all of Google (vetting images to protect child users).
Picktochart. Templates for slide presentations, infographics, and flyers.
Screen castify. Video creator that allows for screen capture and voice recordings.

Tools for Collaboration:
Padlet. Information collection board.
Coggle. Collaborative tool for mind mapping.
Flipgrid. Tool for social collaboration through the use of video.
Zoom. Cloud based video communications platform for video and audio conferencing, collaboration, chat, and webinars.
Google Meet. Video Conferencing app.

Tools for Demonstrating Understanding:
Vizia. Quiz application using content videos.
Kahoot. Quiz application.
Wix. Website or digital portfolio creator. Similar to Weebly.

REFERENCES

Dunlap, J. C., Sobel, D., & Sands, D. I. (2007). Supporting students' cognitive processing in online courses: Designing for deep and meaningful student-to-content interactions. *Tech Trends, 51*(4), 20–31.

Palloff, R. M., & Pratt, K. (2004, August). Learning together in community: Collaboration online. In *20th Annual Conference on Distance Teaching and Learning* (pp. 4–6).http://teacamp.vdu.lt/moodle2/pluginfile.php/1706/mod_resource/content/1/C1NN/Learning_Together_in_Community_Collaboration_Online.pdf.

Palloff, R. M., & Pratt, K. (2005). *Collaborating online: Learning together in community* (Vol. 32). Jossey-Bass.

Papp, R., & Matulich, E. (2011, December). Negotiating the deal: Using technology to reach the millennials. *Journal of Behavioral Studies in Business, 4*, 1–12.https://www.aabri.com/manuscripts/111063.pdf.

Picciano, A. G. (2018). *Online education: foundations, planning, and pedagogy*. Routledge.

Ritter, C. & Polnick, B. (2008). Connections: An essential element of online learningcommunities. *International Journal of Educational Leadership Preparation, 3*(3), 1–5.

Rodríguez-Ardura, I., & Meseguer-Artola, A. (2018). Immersive experiences in online higher education: Virtual presence and flow. In A. Visvizi, M. D. Lytras, & L. Daniela (Eds.), *The future of innovation and technology in education: Policies and practices for teaching and learning excellence* (pp. 187–202). Emerald Publishing Limited.

Rothkopf, E. Z. (1970). The concept of mathemagenic activities. *Review of Educational Research, 40*(3), 325–336.

Swan, K., Garrison, D. R., & Richardson, J. C. (2009). A constructivist approach to online learning: The community of inquiry framework. In C. R. Payne (Ed.), *Information technology and constructivism in higher education: Progressive learning frameworks* (pp. 43–57). IGI Global.

Vanslambrouck, S., Zhu, C., Pynoo, B., Lombaerts, K., Tondeur, J., & Scherer, R. (2019). A latent profile analysis of adult students' online self-regulation in blended learning environments. *Computers in Human Behavior, 99*, 126–136.

Vesely, P., Bloom, L. & Sherlock, J. (2007). Key elements of building online community: Comparing faculty and student perceptions. *MERLOT Journal of Online Learning and Teaching, 3*(3), 234–246.

Vygotsky, L. S. (1978). *Mind in society: The development of higher psychological processes*. Harvard University Press.

Wigfield, A. & Eccles, J. S. (2000). Expectancy–Value theory of achievement motivation. *Contemporary Educational Psychology, 25*(1), 68–81.

Chapter Four

Pedagogical and Andragogical Considerations in Online Teacher Education

Mark M. Diacopoulous and Brandon M. Butler

During Brandon's teaching career, technology was largely a tool students used to produce outcomes of learning, such as activities and assessments. As a social studies teacher, Brandon's pedagogical approach focused on the relational dynamic of teaching and learning, and centered on the use of discussion, project-based learning, simulations, and inquiry, much of which he saw as not needing to rely on technology. When Brandon shifted to teacher education, these instructional orientations followed, even when he was employed by a university with a strong online learning presence.

For several years, Brandon avoided online teaching whenever he could, preferring a face-to-face learning environment he felt best reflected his teaching style and beliefs. However, as he moved toward tenure, he was tasked with overhauling an outdated master's program for already licensed teachers into an asynchronous online format. Brandon was able to conceptually orient the program around his commitment to reflective practice and practitioner inquiry, and he was mindful of best practices of programmatic design such as the incorporation of cohort-based learning.

However, as the director for this newly revised program, Brandon also had to lead the design and instruction of several courses that reflected the program's orientation toward reflection and inquiry, concepts of which Brandon had deep professional knowledge.

But how would these courses "look" in terms of design and enactment? Thinking from the perspective of a face-to-face instructor, Brandon was concerned about the absence of the deep three-hour discussions and learning activities that would normally take place on a weekly basis. In such a space, students are able to collaboratively problem-solve in real time and learning could be scaffolded in class meetings.

For Brandon, he was worried about what an online course format would look like for classroom teachers learning about, for example, reflective practice and practitioner inquiry? As someone who facilitated classroom discussion and learning activities, what was to be Brandon's role in an asynchronous learning environment beyond instructional designer and assessor of learning? Brandon would come to find the answers in andragogy and the dispositions and skills of online teaching and learning.

In this chapter the authors examine the critical concepts at play when designing or redesigning courses for online instruction. From the vignette, we can see that Brandon faced a dilemma when asked to move his classes to an online environment. Brandon was concerned that by moving online, the ability of his students to collaborate, communicate, and critically think in a meaningful manner would be severely compromised.

Brandon's predicament is no doubt familiar to anyone charged with creating online courses. Effectively, Brandon faced a dilemma centered around issues of pedagogy and andragogy. In considering solutions to his problem, he was compelled to consider his skills, knowledge, and dispositions toward online learning. In wrestling with these issues, he realized that he ultimately needed to define a rationale, or purpose, for teaching the course before he could begin course design.

This chapter, therefore, will discuss issues of pedagogy and andragogy when teaching online. Some of the key skills, knowledge, and dispositions necessary to teach in an online environment will be outlined. The chapter will conclude with a series of recommendations or key considerations for teacher educators to think about when designing online instruction.

CRITICAL QUESTIONS

In order to understand the issues of pedagogy and andragogy, and how they influence online instruction, this chapter will answer four critical questions. These questions are:

1. What skills and knowledge do I need to teach online?
2. What dispositions should I cultivate when teaching online?
3. What should skill, knowledge and dispositions look like when teaching online?
4. Where do I start?

DEFINING PEDAGOGY AND ANDRAGOGY

At the heart of all instruction (i.e., online, face-to-face, or hybrid) are issues surrounding the pedagogical and andragogical approaches we take as instructors. These terms are at times misunderstood and used interchangeably, so working definitions are provided for you:

Pedagogy

In education literature, "pedagogy" is often used as a catch-all term to describe the methods teachers employ in the classroom. There is a technical dimension to pedagogy which is important when working with children and adults. For example, we often label instructional strategies and approaches to classroom management as pedagogy. However, using the term in this manner can be overly simplistic.

Van Manen (1994) states that pedagogy implies "distinguishing between what is appropriate, inappropriate, good or bad, right or wrong, suitable or less suitable for children" (p. 139). The relational nature and moral aspect to van Manen's definition reflects a commitment of the teacher to an interest in "children's education and their growth toward adulthood" (p. 139). Using this definition, pedagogy is about more than instructional practice; it describes the relationship between teacher and learner with a focus on the responsibility of the teacher to do what is best for the child. This definition effectively means that decisions made by an instructor should be centered around doing what is best to meet the needs of the learners in the class.

Andragogy

If pedagogy is instruction centered around doing what is best for the child, andragogy addresses a slightly different approach necessary to account for the needs of adult learners. Developed by Knowles (1984), andragogy is based on five assumptions:

a. Adult learners are self-directed learners;
b. Adult learners bring a wealth of experience to the educational setting;
c. Adults enter educational settings ready to learn;
d. Adults are problem-centered in their learning; and
e. Adults are motivated by internal factors.

Knowles further outlines key steps an instructor should take to capitalize on these assumptions. These steps include:

a. creating a cooperative learning climate;

b. planning goals mutually;
c. diagnosing learner needs and interests;
d. helping learners to formulate learning objectives based on the needs of individual students;
e. designing sequential activities to achieve these objectives;
f. carrying out the design to meet objectives with selected methods, materials, and resources; and
g. evaluating the quality of the learning experience for the learner that included reassessing needs for continued learning.

Therefore, andragogical assumptions need to be used as a starting point for approaching the adult online learning environment (Blondy, 2007).

When considered alongside van Manen's (1994) definition of pedagogy, there is a case to be made that online instruction should follow a learner-centered, constructivist approach that fosters relationships and engages learners in the learning process (Bailey & Card, 2009). The interplay between pedagogy and andragogy forms the basis from which the critical questions evolved. However, in order to fully answer these questions, instructors must examine the skills, knowledge, and dispositions needed to develop and facilitate their online instruction and course design.

KEY ATTRIBUTES FOR TEACHING AND DESIGNING ONLINE COURSEWORK

Skills

The practice of learning to teach online is described as a "haphazard, often trial-and-error process" (Schmidt et al., 2013, p. 139). However, researchers have described the skills needed to teach online. For example, Cyrs (1997) described several competencies needed to teach in a virtual environment. These competencies include:

- course planning and organization;
- verbal and non-verbal presentation skills;
- use of questioning strategies; and
- coordination of student activities across multiple sites.

Pelz (2004) further argues that strong online instructors designed courses which addressed cognitive, social, and teacher presence, with the instructor able to project themselves into the learning community. McCombs and Vakili (2005) named four factors for effective online instruction:

- instructor interaction,

- student-centered learning environment,
- time-on-task, and
- quality interactive learning activities.

While Kyong-Lee and Bonk (2006)[AU: **Please add this source to the References.**] conclude that teaching strategies, course design, and online teaching skills are important for quality online education. Finally, Kirwan and Roumell (2015) proposed a list of roles for online instructors:

- professional,
- pedagogical,
- social,
- evaluator,
- administrator,
- technologist,
- advisor/counsellor, and
- researcher.

Ultimately, these skills rest on a foundational basis of knowledge unique to an online instructor.

Knowledge

The Technological, Pedagogical, and Content Knowledge (TPACK) framework (Mishra & Koehler, 2006) describes the complex interplay between the three types of knowledge necessary for a teacher to teach with technology. This interplay includes the people teaching or designing online courses. Mishra (2019) recently updated the model to include Contextual Knowledge as a domain surrounding the TPACK model (see figure 4.1).

Technological Knowledge (TK). In the context of teaching online, Technological Knowledge (TK) refers to the instructor's familiarity with the method of course delivery. For example, an instructor's ability to design and deliver a course within a Learning Management System, if one is used, rests in this domain. Likewise, an instructor's familiarity with Web 2.0 tools that can facilitate student learning, or help with productivity outside of the learning management system would also comprise technological knowledge.

Pedagogical Knowledge (PK). In the context of teaching online, Pedagogical Knowledge refers to the instructor's ability to address issues of pedagogy and andragogy as discussed earlier. For example, the instructor's ability to facilitate a learner-centered approach to instruction, which also meets the diverse needs of the students and maintains motivation and engagement, would reside in this domain.

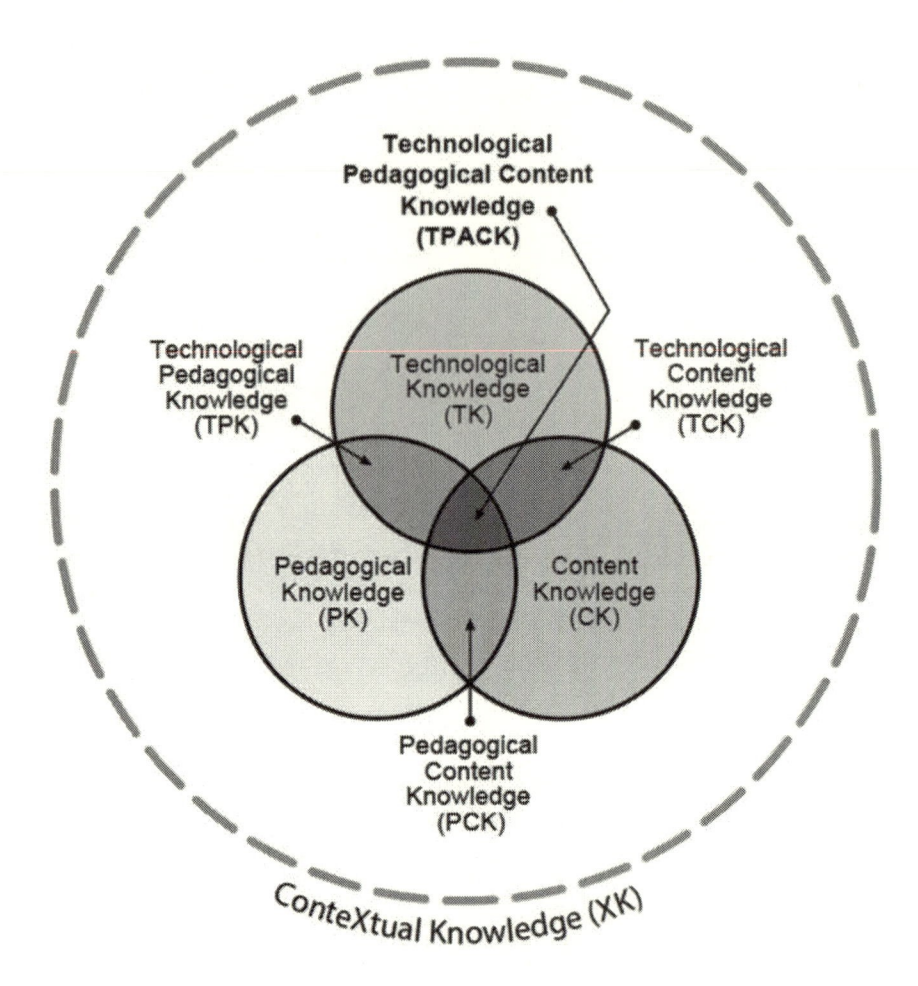

Figure 4.1. Technological, Pedagogical, and Content Knowledge + Contextual Knowledge. TPACK+XK. (Mishra, 2019). The TPACK+XK model is most helpful when examining the skills needed to design and teach an online course.

Content Knowledge (CK). In the context of teaching online, Content Knowledge refers to the instructor's level of familiarity or expertise in the content being taught. (Content familiarity and expertise is addressed in more detail in chapter 3.) Presuming the instructor possesses the required level of technological and pedagogical knowledge to manage and deliver an online course, the instructor must also possess sufficient content knowledge so that they can support and facilitate learning in this course.

Contextual Knowledge (XK). Contextual knowledge is described by Mishra (2019) as "everything from a teacher's awareness of various technologies, to the teacher's knowledge of a school, district, state, or national policies they operate within" (p. 76). These situational contexts relate to the ways the course is delivered. A solid understanding of the contextual factors surrounding the online course is essential if instructors are to successfully combine technological, pedagogical, and content knowledge, in the design and delivery of their online instruction.

Dispositions

Dispositions are the precursors to a teacher's behaviors (Thornton, 2006). For an online instructor to foster the key skills of Technological, Pedagogical, and Content Knowledge (TPACK) previously described, they first need to develop key dispositions necessary for online instruction and course design.

In the context of online instruction, dispositions are the enactment of traits, values, and behaviors in context (Carroll, 2012)**[AU: Please add this source to the References.]**. For example, Welch et al. (2014) claim that empathy, timeliness, and passion are fundamental attributes necessary for online instruction. These qualities could be seen as a focus on meeting student's needs, giving feedback in a timely manner, and showing a dedication for the content and the processes of learning.

Other researchers focus on three key areas in which teacher dispositions manifest in online learning: engagement, meeting learner's needs, and online dialogue.

Engagement. Engagement occurs when course members interact with course material, or when course members interact with each other (Chametzky, 2013). In a face-to-face environment, engagement can be controlled, encouraged, and facilitated by the instructor. Indeed, the personality of the instructor and how they teach directly influences the level of engagement.

Online instructors should have "presence" in the course, a goal that instructors often find challenging in order to strike the right balance. They must prevent their personalities from dominating in an online course (Kirwan & Roumell, 2015). To mitigate this challenge, the course itself should be engaging. Chametzky (2013) suggests one way to accomplish this outcome is to use course materials which are relevant to the learners. He explains that if learners can relate the course materials to some aspect of their lives, then the materials will go some way to engage the learners.

Another way would be to encourage more collaborative activities in which the learners engage with each other. However, collaborative activities sometimes require a rethink of grading systems and policies to ensure equity. Palloff and Pratt (2009) suggest using a two-grade system wherein peer group members rate each other's contribution via a rubric, providing the first grade, while the instructor provides the second grade based on the product.

Engagement might also be improved by making the course and coursework meaningful to the students. Engagement might be achieved by adopting an inquiry stance, where instructors canvass learner's understandings and opinions about topics before the formal instruction begins, or by providing opportunities for learners to apply their knowledge in a "real world" context, which goes beyond a graded assignment.

Meeting Student Needs. Similar to Maslow's (1967) hierarchy of needs. There are certain conditions that need to be met before online instruction can begin. For example, course materials need to be readily available to learners and focused on the meaningfulness of the task at hand (Gutierrez et al., 2010). In successful courses, instructors and students should presume course materials are ready from the first day of the class.

Instructors should also test out technology to ensure all connections are working before the class starts. Preparation is important when using websites or tools which operate outside the learning management system. Some tools only work with certain browsers or with specific devices. If learners do not have the appropriate hardware or software, the chosen course materials become irrelevant.

Moreover, learners should be given the chance to explore the resources and tools in non-graded activities in order to increase familiarity and reduce anxiety. Developing rubrics to accompany each graded assignment is highly recommended, thereby decreasing anxiety and allowing for greater transparency (Palloff & Pratt, 2009). Learner expectations should align with their experiences (Kilie-Cakmak et al., 2009). In turn, learner's experiences should align with the instructor's objectives.

Online Dialogue. While many online instructors did not mature in a digital culture, digital communication is likely to be a normal or even preferred communication for online learners. Creating and sustaining relationships in the absence of face-to face interaction can be challenging (Gilbert et al., 2013). Furthermore, many learners identify online mediums as a gateway to community and not as an obstacle to community building. Thus, the goal for instructors is to facilitate online instruction to create meaningful dialogue (Notar et al., 2005).

Instructors should be creative in their approaches. For example, using video-conferencing, online discussion tools, and giving feedback by video chat can replace face-to-face models of instruction and dialogue (Schmidt et al., 2013). Likewise, instructors should model multiple methods of digital communication for "office hours" or out of class communication. This expectation could include maintaining a digital backchannel which keeps the instructor and learners connected throughout the duration of the course (Carpenter & Green, 2017).

SUMMARY

As instructors, how we enact our understanding of pedagogy and andragogy reflects our knowledge, skills, and dispositions. This chapter makes a case that teaching and designing online instruction requires a student-centered pedagogical and andragogical stance. Instructors and course designers should display a willingness to become technologically adept enough to navigate the learning management system, or other method of delivery. Furthermore, instructors should ensure the technology works for their students before the course begins. They should also be, at a minimum, familiar with the materials used in the course prior to commencement of the course.

On a larger scale, instructors need to be aware of administrative and programmatic matters pertaining to the course. This expectation is especially important for new or adjunct faculty. They should also try to get to know their learners, understand what their motives and expectations are for taking the course. The assignments delivered should be engaging and relevant to learners. Ultimately, assignments should have application and use outside the confines of the course. Instructors should aim to design courses which provide as much opportunity as possible for profound online dialogue, collaboration among learners, and assignments which reflect meaningful engagement.

Designing meaningful and high-quality online learning experiences takes time and consideration. From developing a rationale to strengthening one's skills and dispositions, to designing and implementing the course design for the first time should take approximately eighteen months. This process should not be rushed. However, if placed in a situation like Brandon's but with less time, we still recommend consideration of the reflection questions at the end of this chapter.

REFLECTION

Let us revisit Brandon's dilemma of course design and how he was pedagogically and andragogically mindful during that process. A primary concern was the relational dynamic of pedagogy. Therefore, in each of the courses Brandon designed for the program he provided students with opportunities to regularly discuss problems of practice and course content through an online video tool (e.g., FlipGrid). Additionally, students consistently engage in peer review of student work, complete several assignments collaboratively, and in an early course in the program students and instructor write educational autobiographies that are shared with others.

Brandon has designed these courses with andragogy at the forefront. Rather than identifying specific topics to address that may differ on a week-

to-week basis, courses are organized around a central assignment that will help them in their work as educators and/or for degree completion. For example, in the master's program students must complete a practitioner inquiry project. Brandon constructed the content of the practitioner inquiry course around the production of a project proposal, with each module scaffolding student learning sequentially starting with topic proposal, literature review, method proposal, research plan, and concluding with the final proposal.

From an andragogical perspective, teachers in the courses used their individual educational settings, experiences, and interests to determine the topics they addressed in course assignments. Teachers identified problems that existed in their educational contexts they wanted to solve. Brandon also assisted teachers in developing their goals through regular one-on-one video conference meetings. These meetings helped Brandon diagnose the needs and interests of teachers and direct them toward specific resources and learning opportunities.

Such a course design alleviated Brandon's concern of being simply an evaluator. Regular meetings and feedback necessitated engagement and a presence in the learning space, and a mindfulness toward the form and function of feedback provided and questions posed to students.

CRITICAL QUESTIONS ANSWERED

As Brandon's experiences demonstrate, there were many factors for him to consider when designing his course. Ultimately, it was his rationale, or purpose, to maintain the relational dynamic of pedagogy online, at a similar level to the relational pedagogy in his face-to-face instruction. With that purpose in mind, he was able to consider the issues of pedagogy and andragogy as described in this chapter. Therefore, using Brandon's experiences, and the information in this chapter, the critical questions can be answered with the following recommendations for others who are looking to design, or redesign courses for an online or hybrid environment.

What skills and knowledge do I need to teach online?

Technological

1. Get familiar with your Learning Management System (LMS), whether your institution uses Blackboard™, Canvas™, Schoology™, or free-to-use suites such as Google Classroom. It helps to learn how assignments are turned in, how assessment happens on the platform, and how units or modules of instruction can be created, amended, or deleted.

2. Take advantage of training or professional development opportunities offered at your institution. Alternatively, watch free instructional videos or webinars offered by your LMS. Six hours of training can make a huge difference.
3. Become familiar with other online technologies that might help teach the course. Online texts, videos, or Web 2.0 collaboration tools should be tested before they are included. Check for compatibility issues between devices, browsers, your network, and Learning Management System. Ensure learners can access all course materials.

Pedagogical

4. Take time to organize your course from start to finish. Have it online and available to learners from day one of the course.
5. Consider assignments which lend themselves to inquiry learning. Use performance-based assessments, supported by rubrics where possible. Avoid "busy work" with little meaning or relevance.

Content

6. Know your content before you teach the course. This sounds obvious, but learners can tell when an instructor is not confident with the material. At a minimum, make sure you have consumed the same learning materials your learners will during the course.

Contextual

7. Be familiar with the context in which your course is delivered. What level are the learners? Where are they in the program? Have a clear idea about what the course is preparing the learners for next.
8. Know the administrative hierarchy in your department. This is important if you are teaching a course for the first time, or serving as an adjunct. Find a "go to" person for answers to questions of bureaucracy.

What dispositions should I cultivate when teaching online?

Engagement

9. Ensure your coursework is purposeful and engaging. Assignments should be relevant to the lived experiences of the learners. Give learners opportunities to relate their work to authentic contexts outside the confines of the course.

Meeting Student Needs

10. Try to get to know the unique circumstances and motivations of each learner. Help them to get to know you and your expectations as an instructor, while you get to know their expectations from the course.

Online dialogue

11. Facilitate varied opportunities for discussion and collaboration. Use digital tools to foster connections between the learners and the instructor. If possible, go beyond the discussion board as a tool for dialogue. Use video chat or other collaborative Web 2.0 tools.

What should skills, knowledge, and dispositions look like when teaching online?

12. The course should reflect all of the above by being organized into modules, or units, which follow a clear learning path. Each unit should allow for learners to be engaged, meet their diverse needs, but also practice collaboration and discussion.

Where do I start?

13. Begin with a clear rationale, or purpose for the course. Set the objectives with this purpose in mind.
14. Decide what the culminating performance task will demonstrate. Make sure the culminating performance task aligns with both your rationale and the course objectives.
15. Design units or modules which help the learners work toward completion of the culminating task. These units or modules should be the stepping stones the learners need in order to demonstrate success or proficiency in the course.

Once the course is delivered for the first time, instructors find it worthwhile to consider feedback given by the learners, whether officially in course evaluations, or unofficially through informal polls and surveys. Take some time to reflect upon whether the course outcomes truly reflected the rationale you set at the beginning. In turn, consider if the performance task and assignments aligned with both the course objectives and your rationale. Use this reflection to guide future iterations and modifications to the course as you continue to consider issues of andragogy and pedagogy in its design and delivery.

REFLECTION QUESTIONS

1. How does my regular instruction reflect the learner-centered approach to pedagogy and andragogy as outlined in this chapter?
2. Are there philosophical instructional shifts I should consider before I transition to an online learning environment?
3. How comfortable am I with the need to foster the dispositions mentioned in this chapter (e.g., engagement; meeting student needs; promoting dialogue) in my course design?
4. Are there areas of the TPACK framework I need to strengthen in my own instruction?
5. To what extent am I familiar with my institution's digital and bureaucratical infrastructure? How does the infrastructure impede or support my ability to design online instruction?

RESOURCES

Table 4.1 outlines some of the digital resources the authors have used when designing and redesigning online courses. As with all digital resources, names, uses, monetization, and availability are all subject to change. While these resources are familiar, we acknowledge that other tools and resources are also available.

Table 4.1. Digital Resources for Online Courses

Purpose	Resource	Notes
Organize and Deliver Course Content (Licensed by Institution)	Learning Management Systems	Blackboard™ www.blackboard.com Instructure Canvas™ www.canvas.instructure.com Schoology™ www.schoology.com Desire to Learn (D2L)™ www.d2l.com Moodle www.moodle.org (Nnote that these tools are often licensed to institutions. However, Moodle has a limited free version available for educators.).
Organize Course Content and Delivery (No cost)	Google Classroom™ Edmodo™	www.classroom.google.com www.edmodo.com
Online discussion and Dialogue	FlipGrid™ Padlet™	www.flipgrid.com FlipGrid™ is a free- to- use video discussion board.

Purpose	Resource	Notes
		www.Padlet.com Padlet™ is a digital collaboration tool where students can share multimedia resources in a digital space.
Teacher Presence and Content Delivery	Screen capture and video recording software.	Screencastify™ www.screencastify.com Screencastomatic™ www.Screencast-O-Matic.com www.edpuzzle.com
Embed questions into videos	Edpuzzle™	www.edpuzzle.com
Class Communication	Remind™ Talking Points™	www.remind.com www.talkingpts.org

REFERENCES

Bailey, C. J., & Card, K. A. (2009). Effective pedagogical practices for online teaching: Perception of experienced instructors. *Internet and Higher Education, 12,* 152–155.

Blondy, L. C. (2007). Evaluation and application of andragogical assumptions to the adult online learning environment. *Journal of Interactive Online Learning, 6*(2), 116–130.

Carpenter, J., & Green, T. (2017). Connecting and engaging with students through GroupMe. *TechTrends, 61*(1), 89–92.

Carroll, D. (2012). Examining the development of dispositions for ambitious teaching: One teacher candidate's journey. *The New Educator, 8*(1), 38–64.

Chametzky, B. (2013). What is involved in meaningful E-Learning? *Journal of Interdisciplinary Collaboration, 1,* 41–59.

Cyrs, T. E. (1997). Competence in teaching at a distance. In T.E. Cyrs (Ed.) *Teaching and learning at a distance: What it takes to effectively design, deliver, and evaluate programs* (pp. 15–18). Jossey-Bass.

Gilbert, M. J., Schiff, M., & Cunliffe, R. H. (2013). Teaching restorative justice: developing a restorative andragogy for face-to-face, online, and hybrid course modalities. *Contemporary Justice Review, 16*(1), 43–69.

Gutierrez, C., Baralt, S., & Shuck, B. (2010). The integrated process of engagement in adult learning. In M. S. Plakhotnik, S. M. Nielsen, & D. M. Pane (Eds.), *Proceedings of the 9th Annual College of Education & GSN Research Conference* (pp. 33–39). Florida International University.

Kilie-Cakmac, E., Karatas, S., & Ocak, M. (2009). An analysis of factors affecting community college students' expectations one-learning. *Quarterly Review of Distance Education, 10,* 351–363.

Kim, K-J., & Bonk, C. J. (2006). The future of online teaching and learning in higher education: The survey says. *Educause Quarterly, 29*(4), 22-30.

Kirwin, J. R., & Roumell, E. A. (2015). Building a conceptual framework for online educator dispositions. *Journal of Educators Online, 12*(1), 30–61.

Knowles, M. S. (1984). *Andragogy in action.* Jossey-Bass.

Maslow, A. (1967). A theory of metamotivation: The biological rooting of the value-life. *Journal of Humanistic Psychology, 7,* 93–127.

McCombs, B. L., & Vakili, D. (2005). A learner-centered framework for e-learning. *Teachers College Record, 107,* 1582–1600.

Mishra, P. (2019). Considering contextual knowledge: The TPACK diagram gets an upgrade. *Journal of Digital Learning in Teacher Education, 35*(2), 76–78.

Mishra, P., & Koehler, M. J. (2006). Technological pedagogical content knowledge: A new framework for teacher knowledge. *Teachers College Record, 108*(6), 1017–1054.

Notar, C. E., Wilson, J. D., & Montgomery, M. K. (2005). A distance learning model for teaching higher order thinking. *College Student Journal, 39*, 17–25.

Palloff, R., & Pratt, K. (2009). *Assessing the online learner: Resources and strategies for faculty.* Jossey-Bass.

Pelz, B. (2004). Three principles of effective online pedagogy. *Journal of the Asynchronous Learning Network, 8*(3), 33–46.

Schmidt, S.W., Hodge, E.M., & Tschida, C.M. (2013). How university faculty members developed their online teaching skills. *The Quarterly Review of Distance Education, 14*(3), 131–140.

Thornton, H. (2006). Dispositions in action: Do dispositions make a difference in practice? *Teacher Education Quarterly, 33*(2), 53–68.

Van Manen, M. (1994). Pedagogy, virtue, and narrative identity in teaching. *Curriculum Inquiry, 24*(2), 135–170.

Welch, A. G., Napoleon, L., Hill, B., & Roumell, E. (2014). Virtual Teaching Dispositions Scale (VTDS): A multi-dimensional instrument to assess teaching dispositions in virtual classrooms. *MERLOT Journal of Online Learning and Teaching, 10*(3), 446–467.

Chapter Five

Authentic Assessment

Amy E. Thompson and Nancy P. Gallavan

An associate professor preparing K–12 teachers, Veronica has been responsible for a course called Effective Classroom Practices. All candidates enrolled in their college's teacher preparation programs are required to take the introductory course, Teaching as a Profession, and Veronica's course during their first semester in their programs. Effective Classroom Practices focuses on the essential components of curriculum and instruction demonstrated through the preparation and teaching of a lesson plan aligned with the state's teacher evaluation system. Veronica's goals are to enlighten the candidates with the basic knowledge, skills, and dispositions; equip them with purposes, pedagogy, and practicality; and to empower their confidence, competence, and commitment.

The Effective Classroom Practices course is offered only as a face-to-face. Veronica skillfully fulfills the objectives and outcomes scheduled for each class session balanced with allowing opportunities for questions and conversations. From her experiences, Veronica realizes that her candidates may or may not be aware of and/or express all of their concerns. Consequently, she consistently explores ways to extend and enrich class conversations so she and her learners explore efficacy by co-constructing new knowledge and developing new understanding. Likewise, she comfortably and appropriately reroutes her lessons to meet the immediate needs and interests of her candidates.

Clearly, Veronica experiences feelings of success and satisfaction as she ebbs and flows with the candidates in her face-to-face class sessions. However, a faculty member has left the college and the administration wants to move some of their teacher preparation courses online. Veronica has been asked to teach a different course, Assessments and Analysis for Learning, and to offer it via the college's online format.

Although Veronica is well-acquainted with many concepts and practices associated with assessments and analysis for learning, she has not taught this course and she has not taught online. Effective Classroom Practices precedes the Assessment and Analysis for Learning course, so Veronica understands the learners' foundation. The invitation to switch courses and formats sparks Veronica's creativity, so she accepts the challenge.

As Veronica embarks on this new adventure, she realizes she must (a) present all aspects of classroom assessment and data analysis in ways that candidates can easily comprehend with respect for their prior knowledge and experiences; (b) include discussions, activities, assignments, and tests in ways that candidates can contextualize to their current practices; and (c) model the assessments throughout her online course in ways that she and the candidates can co-construct new knowledge to create experiences to use in their own future classrooms.

Accepting responsibility for a new or different course is customary and expected for most teacher educators in higher education. Likewise, offering courses via online teaching and learning has become more common for assorted reasons, generated by choice and by chance. As teacher educators expand their repertoire, they apply their expertise to various projects, allowing them to make important discoveries about themselves and their capacities—personally, professionally, and pedagogically. Frequently, teacher educators either accept responsibility for a different course or transition their current course to online teaching and learning. For Veronica, both changes occurred simultaneously.

This chapter describes authentic assessment and analysis for learning applicable to any course and any format (i.e., face-to-face, online, and hybrid). Teacher educators may incorporate the concepts and practices of assessment and analysis shared in this chapter into their courses regardless of content. Additionally, as more teacher educators transition courses to online formats, the guidance and support offered in this chapter will be helpful. Consequently, we have written this chapter integrating both authentic assessment and analysis for learning and effective online teaching and learning.

AUTHENTIC ASSESSMENT IN ONLINE CLASSROOMS

Teacher education courses offered through online teaching and learning may be organized as synchronous, in other words, happens in real time scheduled by the teacher, or asynchronous, happens at any time scheduled by the learner. Assessments in an online classroom can be conducted formally and informally for both synchronous and asynchronous scheduling via discussions, activities, assignments, and tests. Formal assessments may be announced in advance allowing teacher candidates to prepare in various ways. Knowledge, skills, and dispositions relevant to the objectives coupled with the procedures and requirements relevant to the outcomes should be shared with candidates prior to their completing the assessment.

Informal assessments are not announced in advance; informal assessments are conducted in the moment and tend to resemble typical or usual class session interactions. These assessments allow teacher educators to check on candidates' progress and learning related to understanding content relevant at that time and/or from prior learning experiences necessary for learning at that time. Assessments announced in the moment should be used to inform and, perhaps, inspire candidates and teacher educators as well as to supplement overall course progress and understanding.

All assessments should be as authentic or as realistic as possible, replicating real world application of the course content, concepts, and practices. Assessments should engage candidates in critical thinking, decision-making, and problem-solving; involve creativity and innovation; and allow for candidate connections and personalized customization of the objectives and outcomes. Assessments should draw from newly acquired and constructed knowledge, skills, and dispositions to solve more complex tasks. Most important, assessments must be coupled with individualized and meaningful feedback so the candidates are aware of their own understanding and areas needing growth.

Assessments can be conducted three times during every learning experience, i.e., class session, and three times during every unit of learning, i.e., entire course. Moving clockwise around the learning experience or class session assessment cycle (see figure 5.1), preassessments are conducted at the start of the learning experience to preview the objectives, formative assessments are conducted during the activity to showcase comprehension and creativity associated with the objectives, and postassessments are conducted at the end of the learning experience to demonstrate understanding and mastery of the objectives. Essentially, the preassessment and postassessment must assess the same objectives to measure progress and produce data for analysis. Preassessments and postassessments are conducted in isolation for approximately five to eight minutes each; formative assessments are integrated through the activity so the time is more fluid.

Similarly, moving clockwise around the unit of learning or entire course assessment cycle (see figure 5.2), preassessments can be conducted at the start of the unit/course, and postassessments can be conducted at the end of the unit/course. The preassessment and postassessment must assess the same objectives to measure progress and produce data for analysis. Rather than formative assessments, units/courses include summative assessments conducted near the end of the unit/course to showcase integrated outcomes via practical demonstration of learning.

```
┌─────────────────────────┐       ┌─────────────────────────┐
│    3. Postassessment    │───┬───│    1. Preassessment     │
│ (end of learning        │       │ (start of learning      │
│  experience)            │       │  experience)            │
└─────────────────────────┘       └─────────────────────────┘
              ↘                  ↙
              ┌─────────────────────────┐
              │  2. Formative Assessment │
              │     (during activity)    │
              └─────────────────────────┘
```

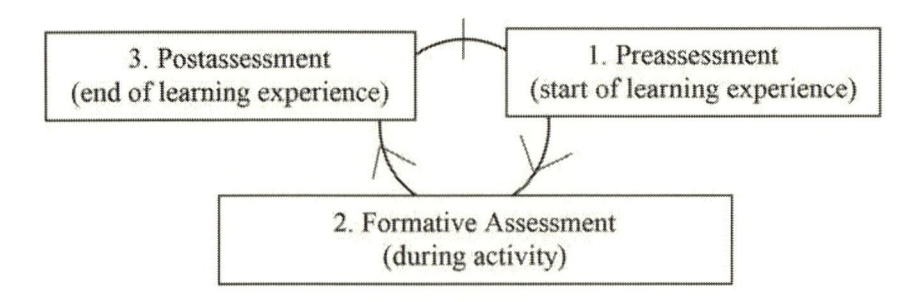

Figure 5.1. Learning Experience/Class Session Assessment Cycle.

Teacher educators are responsible for assessing their candidates' progress and providing them with meaningful feedback throughout the course. Assessment data allow the teacher educator to monitor and measure their candidates' learning cumulatively throughout the course and specifically during each learning experience. Data analyses provide valuable trends that teacher educators should use to align and modify their curriculum, instruction, and assessments immediately to revisit or remediate key information, gradually to increase learning during the remainder of the course, and long term to increase the overall effectiveness of the future offering of the course. With every assessment, teacher educators are responsible for providing every candidate with feedback, i.e., information that is individualized, criteria based, constructive, specific, and motivating. Candidates want to know their levels of success in demonstrating the anticipated outcomes and ways to increase their knowledge, advance their skills, and enhance their dispositions contributing to their personal, pedagogical, and professional efficacy.

FOUR ESSENTIAL ELEMENTS OF ASSESSMENT

Essential for all individual assignments are four elements that must be aligned with the objective and provided for candidates prior to starting the assignment. The four elements include: (a) comprehensive instructions; (b) acceptable sample(s); (c) a detailed rubric with specific criteria; and (d) open-ended spaces on the rubric for candidates to self-assess their product.

First, comprehensive instructions should be written in language that candidates understand and can apply easily. If new concepts, skills, and/or vocabulary are introduced in the instructions, they must be clearly defined, and resources must be provided for candidates to read or view for more information. Teacher educators are strongly encouraged to ask a peer to provide them with feedback on the comprehensibility and clarity of their assignment instructions.

Authentic Assessment 63

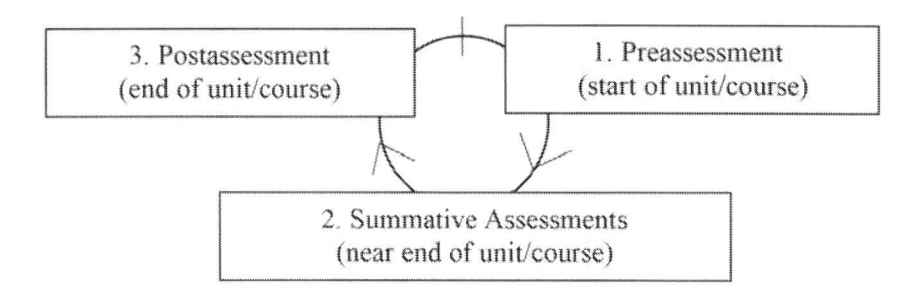

```
┌─────────────────────┐         ┌─────────────────────┐
│  3. Postassessment  │         │  1. Preassessment   │
│  (end of unit/course)│        │ (start of unit/course)│
└─────────────────────┘         └─────────────────────┘
              ┌─────────────────────────────┐
              │  2. Summative Assessments   │
              │  (near end of unit/course)  │
              └─────────────────────────────┘
```

Figure 5.2. Unit of Learning/Entire Course Assessment Cycle.

Second, assignment instructions should be accompanied by an acceptable sample or portions of an acceptable sample to model expectations. Frequently during face-to-face instruction, teacher educators provide samples in class and/or candidates ask if various samples would be acceptable. Posting an acceptable sample of the assignment allows candidates to spend more time on their own construction and creativity rather than wondering about the teacher educator's intention and formatting. Teacher educators should include guidelines on the sample as to which parts of the sample candidates may and may not replicate on their own assignment submissions.

Rubrics

Third, a detailed rubric provides candidates with the specific criteria that the assignment is expected to include. Too often, teacher educators prepare rubrics with three or four general outcomes with each general outcome including multiple criteria. When multiple criteria are grouped together for one general outcome, candidates cannot be sure which criteria were included and/or proficiently and which criteria were not included and/or proficiently. Teacher educators are urged to prepare rubrics with each outcome related to a limited number of, i.e., one or two, specific criteria. Criteria should be listed in the same order that the assignment is written and the teacher educator will score it. Likewise, teacher educators need to consider the way that criteria are grouped regarding the content and the mechanics. The more specific the rubric, the more confident and competent the candidates will be when preparing the assignment. Plus, detailed rubrics make scoring and providing meaningful feedback easier and more efficient for teacher educators.

The rubric should include at least four columns with the first column identifying the expected outcome, the second column identifying the possible points, the third column identifying the candidates self-assessed earned points, and the fourth column identifying the teacher educator's scored points as shown in figure 5.1. Some teacher educators may want to include a peer assessment, so another column can be inserted as appropriate. Including columns for self-assessment increases candidates' attention to each of the criteria and the likelihood that they will proofread their assignment more carefully and better attend to the details. Frequently, candidates will score themselves differently from the teacher educator, which alerts the teacher educator to maintain an open mind and various perspectives and allows an opportunity for open dialogue between the teacher educator and the candidate.

Fourth, the rubric should allow a space at the bottom of the document for the candidate to ask questions and/or share information with the teacher educator. This space should also be used by the teacher educator to provide constructive feedback to the candidate about the assignment. Feedback should be individualized, specific to the assignment criteria, clear, constructive, and motivating for future participation and productivity. Teacher educators should identify the product's greater strengths as well as the weaker strengths (rather than weaknesses). Feedback can include links to resources for candidates to find more information related to both their greater and their lesser strengths. Additionally, feedback can include a link to a tool such as VoiceThread where the teacher educator responds to the assignment via voice rather than in print and then submits that voice response to the candidates as their feedback. See figure 5.3 for a Rubric Template and figures 5.4 abd 5.5 for a Rubric Sample.

ASSESSING ONLINE DISCUSSIONS

In order to provide an authentic assessment of an online discussion and provide each candidate with meaningful feedback, teacher educators must establish the purpose and procedures accompanied by a rubric for the teacher educator and candidates to use for scoring the postings. Just as with activities, assignments, and tests, candidates want to know the expectations and value of each expectation, i.e., number of points possible. We recommend that the rubric for online discussions be generic and apply to all online discussions throughout the course. Candidates like tools and techniques with which they become accustomed to using and can be replicated for use in their own future classrooms. Yet specific expectations related to the content, mechanics, and procedures for each discussion should be incorporated into the rubric. And, as with assignments, providing a sample online discussion posting with a scored rubric will aid in candidates' comprehension of the teacher educator's expectations.

Name of Assignment				
Due Date Submission Process				
Name:		Course:		Date:
Content Modified as needed	Possible Points Modified as needed	Self-Assessment	Earned Points	Feedback
Expectation 1	10			
Expectation 2	10			
Expectation 3	10			
Expectation 4	10			
Mechanics 1	2			
Mechanics 2	2			
Mechanics 3	2			
Mechanics 4	2			
Mechanics 5	2			
TOTAL	50			
Candidate Comments: (required or optional)				
Teacher educator Feedback: (required)				

Figure 5.3. Rubric Template.

Questioning Techniques for Online Discussions

Online discussions can be conducted by posting questions and/or scenarios, i.e., items, in advance or by posing prompts in the moment. Candidates can respond to prompts individually, be assigned to groups, or select their own groups. When grouping, teacher candidates should keep records of group members to ensure that group membership changes throughout the semester so that all candidates interact with all other candidates in the course. Teacher educators have options but must determine in advance if online discussions should require individual candidate responses or group responses.

Posting prompts should be considered carefully. Prompts should align with a specific purpose to help fulfill a goal of the course or an objective of a specific learning experience. Yet prompts should challenge candidate' thoughts, actions, and beliefs in ways that are safe, welcoming, and wanted. Prompts should not be a regurgitation of information but should be open-ended with either multiple correct responses or no set correct response but a sharing of experiences as related to the content. Prompts should incorporate prior knowledge and experiences balanced with new discoveries and inquiries. Prompts and the procedures must be written clearly, promoting motivation, engagement, curiosity, connections, and achievement.

Philosophy of Education Due Date: 5.1.2020 Submission Process: submit Philosophy of Education paper and rubric as two separate documents to Blackboard. Be sure you have typed your name on each document.					
Name: Hunter Tyson		Course: EDUC 1000		Date:	
Content	Possible Points	Self-Assessment	Earned Points	Feedback
Paragraph- Philosophy Introduction; at last three sentences	3			
Paragraph- describe one belief related to your teaching; *describe what it is; explain how it functions; and justify why you have selected it.	9 (three points per prompt)			
Paragraph- describe one belief related to candidate learning; *	9			
Paragraph- describe one belief related to the enterprise of schooling; *	9			
Paragraph; Conclusion; at least three sentences	3			
Philosophy includes at least 5 paragraphs	5			
Each paragraph includes at least 3 sentences	5			
Grammar, Spelling, Punctuation	5			
Name on Philosophy	1			

Figure 5.4. Rubric Sample.

When posting prompts in advance, candidates are expected to respond to the prompt, and frequently, a specified number of other postings within a

Name on Rubric	1			
TOTAL	50			
Candidate Comments: (required or optional)			
Teacher educator Feedback: (required)			

Figure 5.5. Rubric Sample.

given amount of time. Instructing candidates to respond to other postings increases the interactions, engages the learners, and builds community. Notably, the first few candidates posting their responses will be limited in the number of other candidates who have posted their responses. And the likelihood of the same candidates responding to the same candidates increases during the course with candidates responding closer to the due date receiving little to no comments from other candidates in the course.

FlipGrid is a digital alternative to the discussion board. The teacher educator can pose a question and/or scenario, i.e., items, in advance or pose a prompt in the moment either in written form or digitally via a short video. Candidates can respond to prompts individually via video which is limited by the teacher educator from anywhere between two and five minutes. Using this tool, candidates can respond to the instructor and/or other candidates via video thus establishing a virtual discussion. The pressure of writing, not only focusing on content but also on grammar and mechanics, is alleviated through the use of this tool as candidates are encouraged to talk genuinely through their response. Candidates can prepare notes or a script to read if that is important to them, but candidates can also authentically reflect in the moment on a scenario, question, or concept.

Respectful of format, teacher educators are encouraged to stagger the response due dates. All candidates are expected to post their responses to the prompt by the first due date; then all candidates are expected to post their responses to other candidates' responses by a second due date. Additionally, teacher educators can require candidates to respond to different candidates' responses for each discussion through random assignment, by shared interests, and so on. Just as teacher educators would modify seating arrangements and group activities in a face-to-face classroom, teacher educators should modify interactions for their online courses.

Discussions conducted in the moment require teacher educators to be prepared with prompts written in advance of the discussion. Teacher educators should balance fact-seeking prompts with thought-provoking prompts. When posing a prompt, start with the candidate's name so the candidate is listening carefully. This approach will use time more wisely. The teacher educator must be sure that the correct vocabulary is incorporated into the prompt; for example, the prompt should not use vocabulary not yet introduced or emphasized. Discussions are intended to enrich participation and learning effectively. Extending one candidate's response as the next prompt, such as, "tell me more about . . . ," motivates candidates to listen to one another and not just the teacher educator.

Prompts should be relatively short; they should be stated orally as well as in written form. If the discussion is live, use a chat format to post the prompt. Keep in mind that internet connections may not allow for all candidates to hear all parts of the discussion. Model the type and length of responses you are seeking. Some candidates will talk as briefly as possible; other candidates feel more comfortable and may dominate the discussions, just as occurs in face-to-face classrooms. Teacher educators are highly recommended to use a system to select candidates to respond rather than waiting for candidates to jump in or raise their hands. Random online name generators such as Picker-Wheel or Wheel of Names can be used for this purpose. The teacher educator should keep records of candidates' responses, and when discussions cannot include all candidates, the teacher educators should begin with those candidates during the next discussion. If discussion responses are scored, then teacher educators should communicate the expectations, criteria, and possible points prior to the discussion as well as the earned points with feedback after the discussion. No candidate should ever wonder what they learned or what they earned.

ASSESSING ONLINE ACTIVITIES

Individual and group activities are highly effective for building community, engaging candidates in class discussions, extending connections to concepts and practices, and increasing learning. Online activities can be constructed from assigned reading, such as a linked article or website, or viewing videos; online activities can be led during class sessions just as they would be facilitated in face-to-face settings. Online activities include, but are not limited to, blogs, brainstorming, case studies, critiques, debates, energizers, games, group problem-solving, ice breakers, jigsaw, KWL and KWHL (how did you learn), literature reviews, panels, peer editing, presentations, projects, role playing, scavenger hunts, simulations, socratic discussions, and web quests. One such online activity is TedEd. TedEd is a free online site where teacher educators can create a lesson based around a video and assess the learning and participation via multiple choice, short answer, and open response questions. In any of these online activities, candidates can participate individually or in groups, depending on the purpose of the activity and the procedures provided by the teacher educator. And, as with all discussions, assignments, and assessments, expectation criteria and a scoring rubric should be distributed prior to the activity and returned with feedback after the activity.

The following strategies are useful for formal and informal assessments:

- Graphic Organizers or Mind Maps: In many courses, concepts are more easily understood and applied to practices when categorized into various types of graphic organizers or mind maps, such as MindMup, a free online mind map maker. The graphic organizer is posted on the online course platform for candidates to complete while listening to a teacher educator (live or recorded) or as an assessment before or after listening to the teacher educator. The teacher educator prepares the graphic organizer with enough information for the candidate to complete it without difficulty.
- Concept Maps: Concept maps are a specific type of graphic organizer that allow for additional information to be inserted into it throughout one or multiple class sessions/recordings. Concept maps can include some information to help guide candidates as they continue filling in the shapes. Another option is for the concept map to include all of the information and the candidate is expected to reorganize the information accurately and correctly.
- Cooperative Learning: Using one of various ways to group learners, the teacher educator has options by assigning all groups the same task or each group a different task. (Ultimately, either all groups will report outcomes prompted by the same task to expand one idea or each group will report task related outcomes to expand many related ideas.) Each learner in each group is given a specific responsibility with detailed expectations. Ideally, group members should assess themselves individually and as a group. Cooperative learning groups can occur in person or online via tools such as Zoom's breakout rooms.
- Digital Brainstorming: AnswerGarden is a minimalistic, educational brainstorming tool that can be used as a preassessment or formative assessment. A garden can be posted in a tweet, embedded on a website or blog, and/or used as a poll or mind map. Requiring two to three minutes, teacher educators can enter a topic to create a new garden, share the garden with teacher candidates, and the candidates post a two-to-three-word answer. All of the answers begin generating into the shape of a Word Cloud which could be exported into Wordle or Tagxedo to create graphically appealing Word Clouds. As a preassessment, AnswerGarden can be used to establish the knowledge level or background knowledge of a class on a new topic. As a formative assessment, AnswerGarden can be used to generate descriptors of a topic, key events of a main idea, or a response to a question with a multitude of answers.
- Quick Check: Requiring three to five minutes, each candidate is given access to an assessment built into the online platform. The Quick Check

includes no more than five items that can include multiple choice, true-false, fill-in-the-blank, matching, ordering, and ranking. Items can be displayed online in random order so not all candidates will see the same order of items, and given the limited amount of time, candidates will be required to focus and finish the formative assessment.

ASSESSING TESTS

Online teaching and learning formats provide multiple options for preparing and administering tests. In general, the options include multiple choice, true/false, fill-in-the-blank, ordering, ranking, short answer, and long answer or essay. Each option is accompanied with advantages and disadvantages. For multiple choice assessments, all multiple choice items include a stem and alternative answers. Teacher educators must be sure only one alternative answer is plausible or correct. The other alternative answers are called detractors. The stem must be written with clarity, conciseness, and comprehension. When writing the stem and the alternative answers, avoid introducing new language, negatively stated phrases, or words like "all, none, always, never, etc." Additionally, avoid using grammatical clues such as ending the stem with "a" or "an" so candidates can eliminate incorrect answers based on grammar and not knowledge of content, so beginning three of the four answer choices with a vowel and the correct answer with a consonant and ending the stem with the word "a." Also, when writing the alternative answers, avoid using silly or obscure detractors, or phrases such as "all of the above, none of the above," and so forth. Teacher educators must check the alternative answers to ensure they are close to the same length; the tendency is to write longer alternative answers with more details and complexity for the correct answer. We recommend that teacher educators vary the position of the correct answers and be aware if they have unintentionally created a pattern, like a, c, b, d, a, c, b, d. Multiple choice assessment items are the most difficult to write, yet the easiest to score.

Teacher educators must proofread their assessment multiple times, and ask a trusted colleague to complete their assessment prior to administering with their candidates. They should keep in mind that assessments are designed to measure learning, which in turn, measures the teacher educator's teaching of the course content, concepts, and practices.

True/false assessment items also are difficult to prepare; attention to the wording is required. The teacher educator must read and reflect on the wording from multiple perspectives. The safest true/false items focus on a single concept or practice communicated in fairly short sentences, avoiding words like "all, always, some, none, and never."

Fill-in-the-blank items can be prepared with or without providing a possible word list. When a word list is provided, fill-in-the-blank items become matching items. The number of possible words available to use for matching should be greater than the number of blanks to be filled. Additionally, the number of possible words should be listed in alphabetical order and limited to a reasonable and logical number of words developmentally appropriate for the learners. These same suggestions apply to test items employing ordering and ranking assessments.

For multiple choice, fill-in-the-blank, matching, ordering, and ranking assessments, items and answer choices should be randomized. Teacher educators cannot monitor online test-taking, so randomizing items and answer choices requires candidates to think carefully. Fortunately, many online platforms can be set to automatically randomize and score these assessments such as Blackboard, Google Forms, and Socrative. Additionally, Kahoot and Nearpod are equipped in the same fashion with the primary difference being these formats are engaging by providing game-like formats.

For both short and long answer or essay test items, teacher educators must write detailed instructions. If the teacher educator is seeking a specific number of reasons, or examples, then the number must be included in the instructions. Likewise, if the teacher educator is seeking responses with specific vocabulary, concepts, contexts, then these expectations must be stated in the instructions. Teacher educators must read and score candidates' responses to short and long answer or essays carefully. A rubric is highly recommended for these test assessments communicated in the instructions and returned with the score and feedback. Consequently, all requirements being scored in the rubric must be addressed in the instructions and not hidden in descriptors in the rubric.

When conducting online tests, teacher educators must be prepared for situations when candidates cannot access the test (particularly due to the teacher educator's preparation), the technology does not operate throughout the allocated time, the candidate was unable to take the test due to unlimited explanations, and so on. Teacher educators must be ready for reopening tests for specific candidates.

Every assessment enables candidates to monitor and measure their own learning, their understanding and application of the concepts and practices. Concomitantly, teacher educators authentically assess candidate learning and provide meaningful feedback to candidates as teacher educators continuously analyze assessment data and incorporate modifications to their courses.

CONCLUSION

Veronica taught the Assessment and Analysis for Learning for one semester; then, following her own model, she reviewed each assessment and analyzed the data. Reflecting on her first intention, Veronica noted identified concepts and practices that needed to stay, leave, and/or be modified especially in consideration of her candidates' prior knowledge and experiences. When Veronica planned the course, she was limited by her own knowledge and experiences extending from the Effective Classroom Practices course. Now Veronica was attuned to the full range of knowledge and experiences that her candidates brought to the course.

Combining her second and third intention, Veronica realigned the assessment practices used in her course for discussions, activities, assignments, and assessments. Optimizing learning, she varied the types of assessments she used to showcase them for her candidates to use in their future classrooms.

REFLECTIVE QUESTIONS

1. Why should teacher educators conduct assessments?
2. Why should teacher educators analyze data?
3. Why is conducting each of these assessments: preassessments, formative assessments, postassessments, and summative assessments, important?
4. How do the data analysis associated with each of these assessments: preassessments, formative assessments, postassessments, and summative assessments contribute to candidates' learning as well as teacher educators' teaching?
5. What are various ways that teacher educators can conduct assessments in their online teaching and learning?

RELATED RESOURCES

Guidelines with Zoom, WebEx, and other similar real time conversation applications:

- Schedule meetings using the application's tools; email the link to the participants.
- Email documents, links, PowerPoint presentations, and such to participants at least two days in advance of the class session; include special instructions, read in advance of the class meeting, think, and/or prepare an

activity or assignment prior to class session; be sure you can share your prepared activity or assignment during the class session.
- As the teacher educator, familiarize yourself with all the tools and techniques of the application; know the content; have documents ready to share during the class session.
- As the teacher educator be aware of the participants' view of you and your background.
- Begin admitting participants to the class session approximately fifteen minutes prior to the announced starting time; use this time for casual conversations so candidates become more comfortable, can ask the teacher educator questions, and share important information as they are admitted.
- Co-construct netiquette guidelines so all participants can contribute to the class session expectations and interact appropriately; most likely, you will need to gently remind participants about the expectations as everyone becomes more comfortable with the tools and techniques.
- Zoom offers multiple instructional strategies: sharing a document (which allows you to show a prepared document and construct a document in real time); conducting a poll; creating breakout rooms; recording meetings.

ONLINE ASSESSMENT TOOLS

- Answer Garden: https://answergarden.ch; Minimalistic real-time polling and brainstorming tool
- Buncee: https://app.edu.buncee.com/; High engagement to increase creativity through endless possibilities
- FlipGrid: https://info.flipgrid.com; Engaging, accessible, and free tool to make quick videos in response to teacher prompts or as an alternative to discussion boards
- Google Forms: https://support.google.com/docs/answer/7032287?hl=en; Use Google Forms to create, grade, and release results of quizzes
- Kahoot!: https://kahoot.com; User-generated multiple-choice quizzes that can be accessed via a web browser or the Kahoot ap
- MindMup: https://www.mindmup.com; Mind Map maker designed to help focus ideas
- Nearpod: https://nearpod.com; Collaborative activities and formative assessments, like Virtual Reality, Polls, Collaborate Boards, and game-based quizzes
- Peardeck: https://www.peardeck.com/googleslides; Advance use of Google Slides to conduct conversations and assess outcomes
- PickerWheel: https://pickerwheel.com; Randomly choose names

- Socrative: https://www.socrative.com; Interactive, fun, and engaging digital tool that lets you quiz, grade, and assess on the fly
- Tagxedo: http://www.tagxedo.com; Generate word clouds from text
- TedEd: https://ed.ted.com; Create customized video-based lessons with ongoing assessment embedded
- VoiceThread: https://voicethread.com; Replaces text-only discussions and feedback with audio
- Wheel of Names: https://wheelofnames.com; Randomly choose names
- Wordle: http://www.wordle.net; Generate word clouds from text

Chapter Six

Meaningful Feedback in an Online Classroom

Ashlie R. Jack and Shirley Lefever

Bailey is an aspiring candidate in an online teacher education program. She is enrolled in her first semester of college, returning after completing her bachelor's degree ten years earlier, earned by attending an on-campus program. Bailey is returning to school to earn her teaching degree while a full-time, single parent and working 35–40 hours a week.

She is apprehensive about this online platform for learning because she enjoyed the face-to-face interaction with her instructor and classmates during her first degree. She found the brick-and-mortar classroom an environment where she could receive immediate feedback for her thoughts and ideas on the activities and assessments including classroom discussions. She also found time with her classmates an opportunity to receive feedback and a way to gauge her understanding of the book chapter she had just read or the activity, assignment, or assessment she had just completed.

In particular, the dialogue with her professor during class provided an opportunity to gauge her understanding and to ask questions and receive immediate feedback that allowed her to increase her understanding of the information presented in the course. As she entered her first online course, she worried that she would not be able to demonstrate authentic progress or receive meaningful feedback from her instructor or classmates that would allow her to feel confident in her understanding of the course content.

Meaningful feedback can come naturally, almost instinctually, for instructors in a brick-and-mortar classroom. A simple nod of affirmation, eye contact, or a brief comment from a professor can be a powerful reinforcement for learners. When moving to an online classroom, strategies for providing feedback might not always come this naturally. However, if approached with an emphasis on intentionality, meaningful feedback can become a more natural or regular process for any instructor teaching online through a learning management system.

Meaningful feedback is an important aspect of assessment for any learning environment regardless of the delivery mode, online or in a face-to-face classroom setting. Feedback is a part of the learning process that provides guidance to students to deepen their learning, and it allows learners to monitor their performance in a course. Feedback also offers the course instructor the opportunity to assess the effectiveness of the course content they are providing (Cooper, 2016). As illustrated in figure 6.1, feedback supports the learning cycle, and provides opportunities for enhanced academic growth with numerous benefits to the learner.

LEARNING OPPORTUNITIES IN AN ONLINE CLASSROOM

In an online classroom, students have the opportunity to show their understanding of the content through individual assignment submissions, online discussions, online activities, and course assessments. Each of these modalities of learning provide the instructor the opportunity to assess a student's understanding and provide them with meaningful feedback that promotes deep understanding. Meaningful feedback is information provided to the learner based on an assigned task with a focus to improve the learner's performance and understanding of the course content. (Rottmann & Rabidoux, 2017).

Often times, the feedback is based in part on the relationship built between an instructor and a student. Effective educators learn to "read" their students' responses to feedback and adjust their approaches to meet their students' academic needs. For example, some students appreciate public forms of affirmation where others prefer a more private form of guidance. Just as with face-to-face instruction, feedback to the learner in an online environment can be adapted for individual student needs and can occur through written or verbal communication (see the "Related Resources" section below). These high-touch elements of providing written or verbal feedback add a more personalized level of attention to an online course and create a teaching "presence" in an online learning community, which can aid in forming important teacher-to-student relationships. Whether written or verbal, meaningful feedback on assignments should enhance critical thinking, reflective practice, and develop instructor–student relationships (Rottmann & Rabidoux, 2017).

Meaningful Feedback in an Online Classroom 77

Learner Benefits from Meaningful Feedback:
- Increases Motivation & Engagement with Learning Materials
- Allows Learners to Assess Own Progress
- Guides Learner with Self-Improvement
- Encourages Constructive Discussion with Peers & Instructor
- Increases Knowledge Retention
- Promotes Self-Reflection

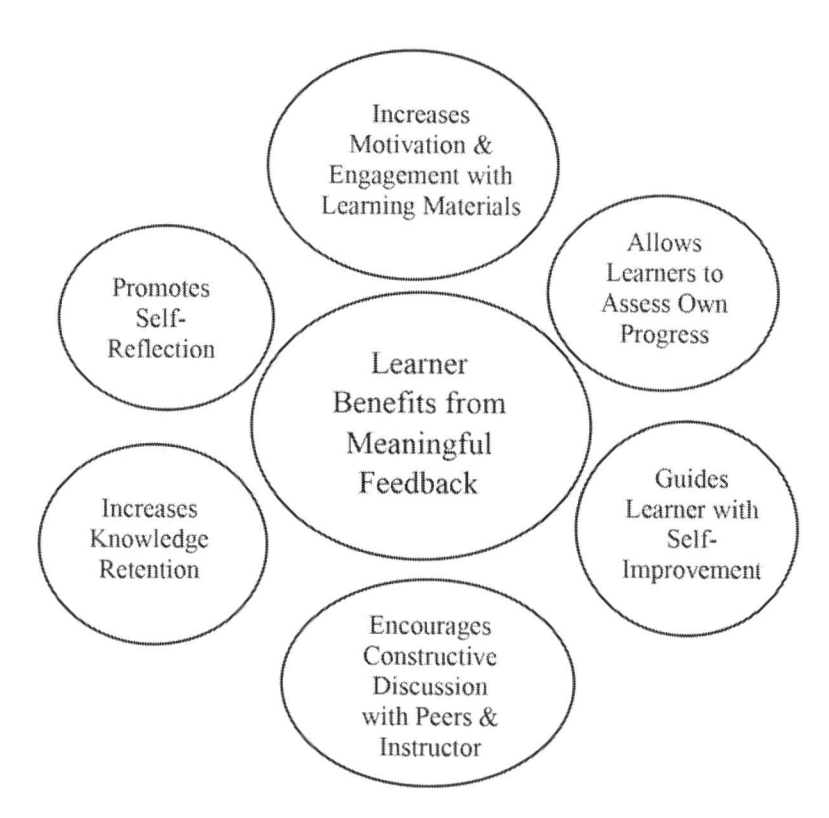

Figure 6.1. Benefits of Meaningful Feedback for Learners. Adapted from "Why Meaningful Feedback Is So Important for Online Learning," by S. Cooper, 2016, ELearning Best Practices (https://elearningindustry.com/meaningful-feedback-online-learning).

FEEDBACK IN AN ONLINE CLASSROOM

Individual Online Assignments

Individual assignments are usually the cumulating piece of a self-paced module that the student has completed. Individual assignment feedback is more than providing a student a total score on their completed assignment. These individual assignments provide the instructor the opportunity to deliver a level of feedback to the learner similar to what they can provide in a face-to-face learning environment.

In order to promote optimal learning and deeper understanding, students need specific and meaningful feedback that encourages them to think critically about their work as well as to reflect on their own learning process. This carefully designed feedback (written or oral) can allow the student to see their own learning in new ways and to gain increased satisfaction from it. It promotes critical thinking and valuable time for guided reflection by the student, and it allows the student to focus on areas they need to improve their work and understanding of the content. In addition, this more individualized feedback can also help promote constructive dialogue between the course instructor and student focused on enhancing the acquisition of the course student learning objectives.

Online Discussions

Building a sense of community is an important aspect of face-to-face classrooms, and is a focus for online courses as well. Many instructors in online courses utilize discussion forums as a means for building this classroom community. These discussion forums help build relationships among all participants and allow instructor-to-student and student-to-student communication to occur. This vital communication is a powerful form of meaningful feedback.

Online discussions are a way for students to post their response to a question or scenario presented by the instructor and allows the other students in the course the opportunity to interact with their classmates through written or oral (video or audio) feedback. Online discussions are a focused dialogue between peers that can scaffold the learning process and allow each student to build on their learning and identify as well as address any misconceptions regarding the course content (Van der Kleij et al., 2017). These online discussion boards replicate the lively discussions that occur in face-to-face classrooms where verbal responses and visual cues provide a student with meaningful feedback.

During an online discussion, both the instructor and students lead the active dialogue. While this dialogue is occurring, the instructor and student responses serve as feedback that is critical *throughout* the active discussion thread versus having to wait until *after* the completion of the discussion to receive meaningful feedback. Online discussion feedback is a social act, a dialogue with and among the students and not a set of independent comments (Ajjawi & Boud, 2017). This feedback reinforces exemplary student performance and guides each student toward a stronger discussion contribution as the active discussion unfolds.

Course Assessments

A frequent tactic for generating course feedback to students by novice online instructors is to utilize the automatic scoring of true/false, matching, and multiple-choice exams. With this feature, a score is immediately generated by the online program and provided to the student when the exam or assessment is submitted. This approach to classroom assessment feedback is limited and does not provide the candidate with the meaningful feedback needed to promote academic growth.

Rather, a course assessment in an online course should provide a candidate with feedback that delivers guidance (written or oral) to the student in order to improve their learning. The level of written or oral feedback provided should give candidates the opportunity to identify and address misconceptions they had on the course material and metacognitively engage the student with the feedback to develop strategies to improve their learning (Hattie & Timperley, 2007).

Instructors who use the course assessment feature can enhance its usefulness in promoting learning by incorporating strategies such as an online discussion following each exam or assessment. Again, this focused dialogue can pinpoint misconceptions and redirect or clarify student understandings. Each of these quick assessments provide the instructor the opportunity to authentically assess student understanding and provide immediate feedback as well as allow the learner to assess their own progress and understanding of the material.

Many students and instructors find online learning intimidating because of the perceived isolated nature of the learning environment. They do not feel an online course can provide the sense of community and connectedness that comes with a face-to face classroom setting. Contrary to this belief, comradery can still exist in an online learning environment by providing authentic assessment that lead to meaningful feedback throughout the course (Rottmann & Rabidoux, 2017). Whether in an individual or group discussion, activity, assignment, or assessment, or course exam, feedback is a crucial component in the online learning environment.

The course instructor and students can utilize written or verbal feedback through a variety of approaches within an online learning management system. The related resources listed at the end of this chapter, available to both the student and instructors, are an avenue for providing meaningful feedback through verbal and video platforms. These resources focus on the use of video and audio to engage students and instructors in conversation *about* feedback. These active and focused dialogues add to the course, which in turn allows both students and teachers to work collaboratively to develop meaning (Hawe & Parr, 2014). This dialogue impacts how effective online teachers structure learning interactions and the feedback with and among students that involves the students as an active agent in the feedback process (Clark, 2012). The key element of feedback is to provide meaningful comments, questions, and dialogue to develop a student's ability to monitor, evaluate, and regulate their own learning (Nichol, 2010; Price et al. 2010).

CONCLUSION

Returning to the vignette provided in the introduction, effective online instruction can alleviate fears faced by many students taking online courses. As Bailey returned to school to complete her professional education coursework, her apprehensions related to learning in an online platform were soon no longer a problem. She quickly found the written and verbal feedback provided on her online assignments, discussions, and assessments by the course instructor and the written feedback she received from her classmates through online discussions, created a beneficial, learning environment much like what she found when attending a brick-and-mortar classroom. Through the clear assessments and focused feedback, which was more than a final grade or score, Bailey discovered that she could self-reflect and grow in her understanding of the knowledge presented in the course and found herself motivated and engaged in the learning process.

REFLECTIVE QUESTIONS

1. How do you ensure you are meeting the academic needs of your online students when assessing them and providing feedback to each student for required online discussions?
2. How do you assess your students and provide meaningful feedback to an online student after the student completes an assignment or assessment through your learning management system?
3. What is your aspiration for integrating meaningful feedback into your online course(s)?
4. Based on the learning management system at your institution, what audio or video approaches will you use to provide your students with meaningful feedback?

RELATED RESOURCES

Resources for Written, Audio, or Video Feedback (adapted from Rottmann & Rabidoux, 2017)

- Jing (https://www.techsmith.com/jing.html) allows the instructor to screen capture a student submission or write instructor comments within the assignment submission and provide verbal feedback to the student in a video format.
- Vocaroo (https://vocaroo.com/) is an audio podcast approach to providing verbal, meaningful feedback to the student through comments about the

submission from the student. A recording link for playback is then linked with the final submission grade provided to the student.
- VoiceThread (http://voicethread.com) is a resource that allows students and instructors to provide written, verbal, and/or video feedback within the learning management system.
- Zoom (https://zoom.us) is a videoconferencing platform that allows instructors and students to conference online for virtual feedback, engage in discussion over assignments, and to clarify content, instructions, and questions. This feedback platform is effective in providing social presence in an online learning environment.

REFERENCES

Ajjawi, R., & Boud, D. (2017). Researching feedback dialogue: An interactional analysis approach. *Assessment & Evaluation in Higher Education, 42*(2), 252–265.

Clark, I. (2012). Formative assessment: Assessment is for self-regulated learning. *Educational Psychology Review, 24*(2), 205–249.

Cooper, S. (2016, August 27). Why meaningful feedback is so important for online learning. *ELearning Best Practices.* https://elearningindustry.com/meaningful-feedback-online-learning

Hattie, J., & Timperley, H. (2007). The power of feedback. *Review of Educational Research, 77*(1), 81–112.

Hawe, E., & Parr, J., (2014). Assessment for learning in the writing classroom: An incomplete realization. *The Curriculum Journal, 25*(2), 210–237.

Nichol, D. (2010). From monologue to dialogue: Improving written feedback processes in mass higher education. *Assessment & Evaluation in Higher Education, 35*(5), 501–517.

Price, M. E., Handley, K., Millar, J., & O'Donovan, B. (2010). Feedback: All that effort, but what is the effect? *Assessment & Evaluation in Higher Education, 35*(3), 277–289.

Rottmann, A., & Rabidoux, S. (2017, September 6). How to provide meaningful feedback online. *Inside Higher Ed.* https://www.insidehighered.com/digital-learning/views/2017/09/06/how-provide-meaningful-feedback-online-course.

Van der Kleij, F., Adie, L., & Cumming, J. (2017). Using video technology to enable student voice in assessment. *British Journal of Educational Technology, 48*(5), 1092–1105.

Chapter Seven

Creating Collaborative Communities in Cyberspace

Lori Fulton and Jon Yoshioka

Deirdre and Allegra were the best of friends, so much alike that they were often mistaken for sisters. They shared everything. So, when Allegra took an online course that she raved about, Deirdre decided to follow suit and enroll in the same course. Their stories unfold below.
Allegra's Story

Allegra, an undergraduate teacher candidate, was extremely apprehensive about taking her required content area methods course. It wasn't so much the course material that bothered her; Allegra was an excellent student, as evidenced by her 4.0 GPA. Rather, Allegra had taken all of her courses in a face-to-face format, and this course was going to be offered completely online. Initially, all of her fears seemed to be well founded. Navigating the tools and platform used for the class appeared to be challenging.

But, instead of suffering in silence, the students got together and presented their concerns to their instructor, Kai, who listened and implemented the changes necessary to help the students succeed. This course, with its robust, active learning community; activities that stretched the students to move out of their comfort zones; collaborative structure, and its instructor, Kai, ended up being the best course Allegra had ever taken. Of course, she wanted to share that rewarding experience with Deirdre.
Deirdre's Story

Deirdre was looking forward to signing up for her online content area methods course after hearing how much Allegra enjoyed her course. While this would be her first experience taking an online course, Deirdre was confident after hearing Allegra's experience that the course would be a good one for her, too. Unfortunately, word had spread and Kai's class was full, but Deirdre found another online section of the course and signed up for it. Deirdre believed that the course she registered for should be just like Allegra's course since all online courses were pretty much the same, right? Unfortunately, that assumption proved not to be the case.

After the first few assignments, Deirdre knew she was in trouble. She was clearly struggling, but why? She was a good student, as evidenced by the "A's" she earned in her face-to-face courses, but she was clearly not doing well in this online format.

Deirdre felt isolated, unsure of assignments, and did not know who to turn to for help. She had signed up for this online course on the recommendation of her trusted friend Allegra, thinking it would allow her to juggle her busy home, work, and school schedules, but instead she found the experience to be not just frustrating, but one that could have a potentially negative impact on her GPA. This experience made her vow to never take another online course again. Deirdre simply could not understand why Allegra had suggested she take an online course and wondered how they could have had such different, totally opposite, experiences with online learning.

ONLINE COLLABORATIVE LEARNING COMMUNITIES

Online courses have grown in popularity, and many individuals have taken an online course at some time in their academic life. As described in the opening vignette, experiences with online courses can span the entire spectrum, from the incredibly positive "Best course I've ever taken in my life" to the incredibly negative "I'll never take any class online again." Which experience was yours? Are you like Allegra, who, by all accounts, had a happy, joyful, and productive experience in her online course, or are you more like Deirdre, whose online experience made her sad, miserable, and frustrated? Which experience will your students have in your online course? How can you create the environment you want your students to experience?

While online courses may have started as readings and online discussion forums, online instruction has evolved to provide platforms and opportunities to create collaborative spaces that promote community among learners. Instructors of online courses can design their courses to help promote a positive online learning experience, one in which the members of the online community engage in structured activities on a variety of levels, including socially, intellectually, and mentally (Tu & Corry, 2003) in order to build a sense of community. The social aspects of learning are recognized to have an impact on learning outcomes (Resnick, 1991) and higher-order thinking (Lipman, 2003) so purposefully structuring activities and strategically providing opportunities to include these various levels of engagement are essential if one is attempting to create an environment where active, collaborative learning experiences can take place.

One major step in creating a positive online learning experience is the development of a collaborative learning community. Collaborative learning has been described as a joint effort to intellectually make sense of new ideas (Smith & MacGregor, 1992). This sense-making process is often a constructivist endeavor, designed around rich contexts, based on the ideas of a diverse group of learners, and carried out in a social manner. Developing this type of community in an online environment has its challenges but is definitely possible.

The ideas of collaborative learning can be traced back to Dewey (1897) who believed that an individual's development was dependent upon the community and Vygotsky (1978) who conceptualized learning as a socially constructed process. Teacher educators must consider how to develop a sense of community and to facilitate collaboration within online courses, how students engage with the ideas of community and collaboration as both learners and teacher candidates, and how students translate their experiences with the learning community to their future classrooms, whether those experiences are face-to-face, online, or hybrid classrooms.

DEFINING COLLABORATION AND COMMUNITY

Collaboration has been defined in many ways, from the simple "the action of working with someone to produce or create something" (Lexico, 2020a) to the more complex "empowering students to deepen the learning experience through their work with one another" (Palloff & Pratt, 2005, xi). Community is defined as "a group of people living in the same place or having a particular characteristic in common" (Lexico, 2020b). With respect to online teaching and learning, the class serves as the common place or characteristic among students.

Collaboration and community go hand-in-hand and it is difficult, if not impossible, to have one without the other as they support one another and work together in a regular, repeated, recurring fashion. The instructor plays an important role in creating a learning environment that promotes a collaborative learning community where students share common learning goals and go beyond them to push the boundaries of learning for one another and themselves. Collaboration also is viewed through the process instructors go through, including stages and tools the instructor can use, in the online teaching and learning environment. When a community collaborates together in these ways, they truly become a collaborative community.

DEVELOPING COLLABORATION: STAGES AND TOOLS FOR COLLABORATION

At the heart of collaboration is the idea that "when I succeed, we succeed" (Palloff & Pratt, 2005, p. 4). However, developing this type of collaborative community takes time and intention on behalf of the instructor, ensuring that activities are connected and intentional, creating a "fully integrated design" (Tu & Corry, 2003, p. 54) for the course. From the early planning stages for the course, the instructor should consider the types of collaborative activities that will be included, how to introduce those activities to students, and how much time is needed to allow students to develop as a collaborative group rather than simply working together to complete a task.

Palloff and Pratt (2005) found that for meaningful and successful collaboration, instructor involvement was essential and followed the sequence of:

a. setting the stage,
b. creating the environment,
c. modeling the process,
d. guiding the process, and
e. evaluating the process.

The first step is to set the stage for collaborative work. The instructor should begin clearly explaining the collaborative nature of the class and why collaboration is important. Next the instructor should establish clear guidelines for activities and ensure that students are comfortable using the technology required in the activity. Setting the stage in this way helps ensure student comfort in the course and allows them to move forward with greater independence.

In creating the environment, it is important for the instructor to ensure that students are provided the time and space to work together collaboratively. Learning to work together collaboratively takes time and is often not accomplished in the span of one online module. It is important to allow for meaningful collaboration between individuals across time and modules (Garrison, 2007).

The third stage is for the instructor to model the collaborative process expected from the students. One example would be to model the types of responses expected in discussions by posing thought-provoking questions that help students connect back to a previous experience. Intentionally modeling the depth and breadth of the types of answers expected would also be beneficial. After modeling, the instructor continues to guide the process by providing feedback. For example, discussions can sometimes take interesting and unexpected twists and turns that might steer the conversation in a variety of different directions. One way to guide a discussion that has strayed from the original focus back to the big idea is to collect quotes from various discussion threads that relate to the big idea to redirect the discussion.

Finally, the instructor must evaluate the process, including asking students to provide feedback on collaborative activities to determine if and how well the objectives were met. Asking students to self-assess their engagement, their aptitude in using the tools required, and their success with the activities can provide valuable information for future assignments and course planning.

In order to carry out these five steps, Palloff and Pratt (2005) described the importance of using tools and techniques to develop a collaborative environment. As with any course, whether online, hybrid, or face-to-face, clarity in instructions and expectations is essential. Instructors must explain how collaboration is defined, how it supports learning, and how it plays a specific role in the course. Collaboration must be clearly articulated and not simply implied.

Furthermore, it is essential that directions for assignments are clear, and online community members know what is expected of each member of the community. Everyone must be aware of the way they can communicate with one another (discussion board, email, phone, etc.) and when each way is most appropriate. The creation and use of agreements and charters also help promote clear guidelines for a collaborative community.

Mutually agreed upon rules for engagement are essential for the smooth functioning of the online community. For example, the group could establish and type up a set of norms and roles and then all community members could sign the online white board to show their agreement, which is similar to the way in which face-to-face classes previously established norms on chart paper, asked everyone to sign, and then posted the results in the classroom. By establishing an agreement such as this at the beginning of the course, it becomes easier to discuss and address issues that might arise if an individual is not fulfilling their role in the collaborative group.

Taking the time to consider the stages and tools required for a collaborative online community can help provide students with a positive experience, such as the one Allegra experienced in her course with Kai. However, reflecting on Deirdre's experience, it is not guaranteed that collaboration between and among class members is going to be present in every class.

Developing the structures and procedures to allow students to effectively engage in mutually respectful, collaborative activities and productive conversations are facets of online teaching and learning that rarely occur without much forethought and planning. Instructors like Kai who thoughtfully and actively seek ways to guide students in building the trust needed to collaborate effectively will likely provide students with opportunities more like Allegra's experiences rather than Dierdre's experiences. Once the foundations for effective collaboration are built, the students and instructor can move on to building an active, thriving, and mutually beneficial learning community.

CREATING COMMUNITY

Once the foundation for meaningful and successful collaboration is clearly established by the instructor and implemented by the students taking part in the learning community, it is possible for students to develop the mechanisms and interactions necessary to work effectively in an online space. This step is essential to the process, as Palloff and Pratt (2005) describe, "collaboration forms the foundation of a learning community online" (p. xi). The idea of collaboration as an essential first step in creating a learning community was further corroborated by Garrison (2007), who noted that more purposeful activities could not be addressed until social relationships were first established.

While it may seem trivial, the time and effort required to develop the social backbone of the learning community is essential in creating an environment that allows students to feel safe and to freely and readily contribute to the group. Once clear guidelines and expectations have been established, mutually agreed upon, and enacted, it is possible to start focusing on the important issues related to forming a community of learners. This process can be aided through:

- The promotion of professional as well as personal exchanges in order to create student commitment and greater enjoyment;
- The creation of a safe and trusting environment in which students feel comfortable about taking risks;
- Affective support between students and between students and lecturer; and
- Commitment of time from students and lecturer. (Maor, 2003, p. 133)

Unfortunately, helping learners become more knowledgeable is not as simple as pouring knowledge into an empty learner vessel, but rather something that requires intentionality and forethought on the part of the instructor in constructing engaging and worthwhile experiences for their online learners. Simply put, as Palloff and Pratt (2005) so eloquently stated, "read and discuss online classes are no longer seen as the best way to deliver content" (p. 4).

First is the realization among the instructor and students that the process of creating, maintaining, and growing a thriving online community takes time. Lots of time. This is not to say, though, that simply adding time to an online class will miraculously create community because it does not. It is clearly not that simple and definitely not a "one and done" situation. Shea

(2006) found no evidence that "courses that are of longer duration resulted in a better sense of learning community" (p. 42).

In order to create, maintain, and grow the relationships necessary for the trust and respect needed to develop between online participants to form into a community of learners, carefully and intentionally selected activities must be provided throughout the class. For example, gradually scaffolding the difficulty of the experiences and activities or gradually taking students out of their comfort zone can result in building stronger bonds between all participants.

If the class involves teacher candidates who are in the field, the instructor could have everyone record a short clip of them teaching. Seeing oneself teach is normally not an easy or comfortable thing in itself. But having other students, i.e., peers see it and comment on it can be even more uncomfortable. The instructor would need to start with having each student analyze and give feedback on their own lesson. The next time, the instructor could have the students partner with another student to view one another's videos, analyze, and provide feedback about their lessons.

To scaffold this experience further, the instructor could then have students work in small groups to watch a student's video, analyze it, and provide feedback on it. Then finally, the instructor could have the whole class watch a student's video, analyze it, and provide feedback as a whole class. Feedback from activities like this usually tends to start tentatively and with minimal detail but by the second or third time, students are willing to give large amounts of thoughtful, helpful, and appropriate feedback.

Second, but equally as important as time, is the realization that place matters. More specifically, everything associated with place and culture matters when trying to create a collaborative online learning community. Shea (2006) stated,

> The design of online, collaborative-learning environments is founded on the assumption that culture matters, that we live and learn in community for a reason, that community-based living and meaning-making is a reflection, to a large degree, of our unique genetic makeup as a species. (p. 36)

How can we create this sense of place? The simplest way is to include opportunities for participants, including the instructor, to learn more about one another beyond superficial levels. One activity that could create understanding of what people think is important. The students post an artifact that is special to them and relates to their sense of place. The post includes discussion prompted by guiding questions such as: (a) what is the object you brought in, (b) why is that object important to you, (c) how does that object represent you as a learner of _____? To further discussion and encourage interaction among students, follow-up questions might include, how might you connect with another individual based on the object they shared?

Facilitating the artifact activity as one of the first "get-to-know-one-another" type of activities during the initial class session allows both the students and teacher to develop a quicker, deeper understanding of one another by highlighting the importance the specially selected item holds in each person's life. The personal knowledge that is built through activities such as these and other shared experiences allows the learning community to develop the ability to respectfully collaborate with one another.

Finally, Tu and Corry (2003) articulately stated that, "collaborative learning is an artistic rather than a mechanical process" where "instructors shift their authority to the learners" and "provide the foundation and learning structures to guide learners through various learning experiences involving active social interaction by applying modern technology" (p. 52). Collaborative learning is not a facet of online teaching and learning that can be prescribed in a series of step-by-step, how-to manuals. The instructor must be confident enough in themselves and their students to "let go" of control of the learning process and, instead, serve as a guide for the students in their journey through the course experiences, allowing the students to take part in the carefully and intentionally chosen activities to construct their own learning environment.

When educators feature collaboration and community in the courses, it is likely that they will be able to create the type of successful online collaborative learning community described by Tu and Corry (2003) that becomes a place where "community members engage intellectually, mentally, socioculturally, and interactively in various structured and unstructured activities to achieve their common learning goals via electronic communication technologies" (p. 53). Consequently, educators are more likely to have students like Allegra who had a positive experience with online learning versus students like Deirdre who, based on her one experience, vowed to never take an online course again.

SUMMARY

What will help ensure students benefit from being able to participate in a safe, thriving, productive collaborative learning community? Consider Allegra's class and some of the elements Kai put in place that helped create the positive experience Allegra and her classmates had. First, Kai took the approach that collaborative activity was an essential component of the online learning environment in order to promote critical thinking, reflection, transformative learning, and the development of knowledge and meaning (Palloff & Pratt, 2005).

To develop a collaborative environment, Kai placed particular emphasis on investing time at the beginning of the course to ensure that students understood the importance placed on collaborative work. Kai set clear mutually agreed upon guidelines about how collaborative work should be completed and how interactions between community members should occur. Ultimately, collaboratively, Kai and the students created an environment in which all members could connect with one another and engage in the task.

Kai also made sure to model the expectations for the course, such as posting thought-provoking questions within the discussions to help students make connections across ideas or clarify their thinking further. Allegra found this modeling to be especially helpful. She was pushed to reflect on assignments at a deeper level so that she could help contribute to the discussions that contributed to the development of shared understanding. Allegra mentioned all of these outcomes to Deirdre, who reflected on her own experience and realized that, unfortunately, none of these opportunities were present in her online class. Dierdre concluded that mostly likely, the environment was the reason she was struggling.

REFLECTION QUESTIONS

1. What role does collaboration play in your online course?
2. How do you develop opportunities for students to collaborate?
3. How can you as an instructor help your students in your online class create the sense of place that will aid them in creating a positive classroom community?
4. How can you build structures or mechanisms to promote the cyclical nature of community and collaboration within your online course?

RESOURCES

Palloff, R. M., & Pratt, K. (2005). *Collaborating online: Learning together in a community.* Jossey-Bass.

Papadopoulou, A. (2019, October 13). 8 easy ways to build an online learning community (in 2020). *Learn Worlds.* https://www.learnworlds.com/build-online-learning-community/.

Tu., C. H. (2004). *Online collaborative learning communities: Twenty-one designs to building an online collaborative learning community.* Libraries Unlimited.

REFERENCES

Dewey, J. (1897, Jan). My pedagogic creed. *School Journal, 54,* 77–80. http://dewey.pragmatism.org/creed.htm.

Garrison, D. R. (2007). Online community of inquiry review: Social, cognitive, and teaching presence issues. *Journal of Asynchronous Learning Networks, 11*(1), 61–72.

Lexico. (2020a). Definition of collaboration. https://www.lexico.com/en/definition/collaboration.
Lexico. (2020b). Definition of community. https://www.lexico.com/en/definition/community.
Lipman, M. (2003). *Thinking in education.* Cambridge University Press.
Maor, D. (2003). The teacher's role in developing interaction and reflection in an online learning community. *Educational Media International, 40*(1–2), 127–138.
Palloff, R. M., & Pratt, K. (2005). *Collaborating online: Learning together in community.* Jossey-Bass.
Resnick, L. B. (1991). Shared cognition: Thinking as social practice. In L. B. Resnick, J. M. Levine, & S. D. Teasley (Eds.), *Perspectives on socially shared cognition* (pp. 1–20). American Psychological Association.
Shea, P. (2006). A study of students' sense of learning community in online environments. *Journal of Asynchronous Learning Networks, 10*(1), 35–44. 10.24059/olj.v10i1.1774.
Smith, B. L., & MacGregor, J. T. (1992). What is collaborative learning? https://www.evergreen.edu/sites/default/files/facultydeveloping/docs/WhatisCollaborativeLearning.pdf.
Tu, C. H., & Corry, M. (2003). Building active online interaction via a collaborative learning community. *Computers in the Schools, 20*(3), 51–59.
Vygotsky, L S. (1978). *Mind in society: The development of higher psychological processes.* Harvard University Press.

Chapter Eight

Professional Ethics and Pedagogical Integrity

Winnie Namatovu and Nancy P. Gallavan

Adrian, a teacher educator with nine years of middle school classroom teaching experience and a PhD in curriculum and instruction, has been teaching an undergraduate teacher preparation course in classroom assessments online every semester during his five-year career at a large state university. According to his academic mentor and student evaluations, Adrian's online course layout is clear and easy to follow; his course design is sequential and meaningful to the learners; and his assignments are learner-centered and relevant to contemporary classrooms. Throughout every semester, Adrian maintains an electronic folder with the modifications he wants to make to his course before he teaches it again. Highly motivated to continue improving the course and his effectiveness, Adrian grapples with issues of authenticity of the course content, fairness in the class interactions, and usefulness of the comprehensive feedback.

Adrian honors his learners' knowledge, experiences, interests, and, most of all, their time. From his experiences in teaching and learning, he has established three foundations: to provide learners information related to all aspects of classroom assessments; to offer learners access to additional resources from various sites with multiple perspectives; and to create opportunities for learners to express and exchange their individual discoveries with their peers and professionals in the field. At the center of these three overlapping foundations is Adrian's primary principle that every learner is a unique person traveling a unique path guided by unique dreams seeking a unique destination carrying a unique bag filled with unique items (see figure 8.1). Thus, Adrian is attuned to differentiating instruction to optimize the learning for every learner.

Adrian considers the learners in his class not as a group of twenty learners all learning the same content and expressing their learning the same way, but as twenty individual learners worthy of understanding twenty different variations of the content and expressing their outcomes in twenty different ways. Through his approaches using differentiation, Adrian acknowledges that his goal is not only for his learners to increase their awareness and applications of outcomes according to their needs, interests, and experiences, but also Adrian wants his learners to increase their attention to and advocacy for social justice in education. To these ends, Adrian must view all aspects of the classroom assessment course from the individual perspectives of his twenty learners, in the context of their status as teacher candidates enrolled in a teacher education course, and as K–12 classroom teachers preparing for success in their careers as teachers, models, and assessors of K–12 learners traveling on their own lifelong, educational journeys.

Consequently, in his quest to equip, enlighten, and empower his learners with effective classroom assessment, Adrian's professionalism and pedagogy frequently focus on three common overarching questions delving into what outcomes are taught and learned, how are these outcomes taught and learned, and why outcomes are chosen and reinforced, both intentionally and unintentionally. Clearly, Adrian's quandaries apply to all teacher educators tasked with developing and delivering courses especially via online teaching and learning. Every teacher educator must select course content, conduct class interactions, and provide learner feedback. Moreover, since Adrian's course focuses on classroom assessments, he wants to capitalize upon these three issues to both communicate learning outcome measurements and to

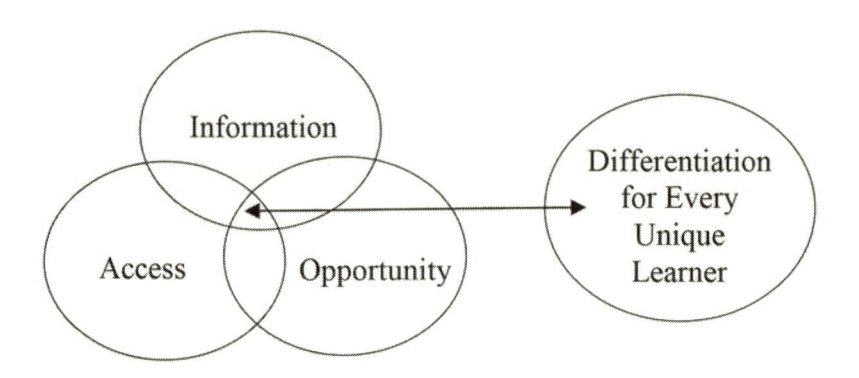

Figure 8.1. Adrian's Three Foundational Beliefs and One Primary Principle. Adapted from "Cultural Competency for Transformative Education," by N. P. Gallavan, 2002, in L. G. Putney and J. Wink, *Visions of Vygotsky* (pp. 157–75).

exemplify effective tools and techniques for providing meaningful and purposeful feedback for his teacher candidates in their K–12 classrooms.

Adrian's challenges with the authenticity of course content, fairness in classroom interactions, and usefulness of comprehensive feedback relate to professional ethics and pedagogical integrity in the context of his goal of effective online teaching and learning. Most likely, teacher educators are superficially acquainted with the words ethics and integrity. Yet many teacher educators do not consider the significant influence of these two constructs for their learners as teacher candidates/classroom teachers and for themselves as teacher educators.

This chapter describes the roles that ethics and integrity play in the development and implementation of course content, facilitation of class interactions, and dissemination of comprehensive feedback. The chapter begins by discussing the meanings of ethics and integrity. Next, the relationship of ethics and integrity is introduced by discussing it in the context of morality and social justice. Finally, there is a discussion around the implications of these four constructs or principles on teacher educators' practices as they relate to Adrian's issues and goals. Within that discussion, the importance of the principles is addressed with respect to teacher candidates' learning experiences in the context of online teaching and learning.

PRINCIPLES OF ETHICS AND INTEGRITY

Ethics

Ethics is defined as "an external system of rules and laws" (Czimbal & Brooks, 2006, para 1), the agreed upon standards identifying desired and undesired behavior, acceptable and unacceptable conduct, and appropriate and inappropriate demeanor considered by a group of people, or organizations, formally or informally (Jensen, 2009). Many organizations have written codes of ethics detailing the minimum standards of conduct, the process for investigating alleged violations, and the corresponding consequences when people within the organization do not comply with the established code of ethics (Czimbal & Brooks, 2006). In general, ethics provide frames of expectations that guide and support both the organization and the people, with appropriate attitudes and acceptable actions, in ways that are applicable to and among the various stakeholders associated with the organization.

Ethics and ethical practices are important to enhance fairness, transparency, trustworthiness, and helpfulness in ways that are easily available for everyone involved in the endeavor (Juneja, 2015). Experiencing the importance of ethics when authentically expressed by both the organization and the people contributes to satisfying the basic human need to feel safe, welcome, wanted, and a sense of belonging. Additionally, ethics and ethical practices create credibility and integrity, unite people and leadership, improve collaboration and decision-making, enhance both short-term results and long-term outcomes, and safeguard individual people, organizations, and society (Juneja, 2015).

Integrity

Integrity is defined as "an internal system of principles" and values (Czimbal & Brooks, 2006, para 1), the beliefs and practices associated for demonstrating profound understanding and strong adherence to ethical and moral expectations (Indeed Career Guide, 2019). Integrity is learned through lived experiences, much like self-efficacy. Bandura (1977, 2000, 2006) identified four sources of self-efficacy: (a) vicarious experiences, i.e., people we watch and hear indirectly; (b) verbal persuasion, i.e., people who instruct directly; (c) mastery experiences, i.e., people who provide opportunities to demonstrate behaviors coupled with feedback; and (d) emotional and physiological states, i.e., the person's own sense of well-being. Perceiving the world around them through these four sources of self-efficacy influences a person's internal understanding of and external actions associated with affective, cognitive, cultural, physical, traditional, and social qualities (see figure 8.2).

Early in life, qualities of integrity contribute significantly to a person's thoughts, actions, and beliefs evident in critical thinking, problem-solving, decision-making, and individual interactions. As people grow, mature, and develop, they realize that they know and are known by their integrity through their demonstrations of wisdom, strength, courage, and justice (Mintz, 2017)

Vicarious Experiences	Verbal Persuasion	Mastery Experiences	Emotional and Physiological States
• Affective • Cognitive • Cultural • Physical • Traditional • Social			

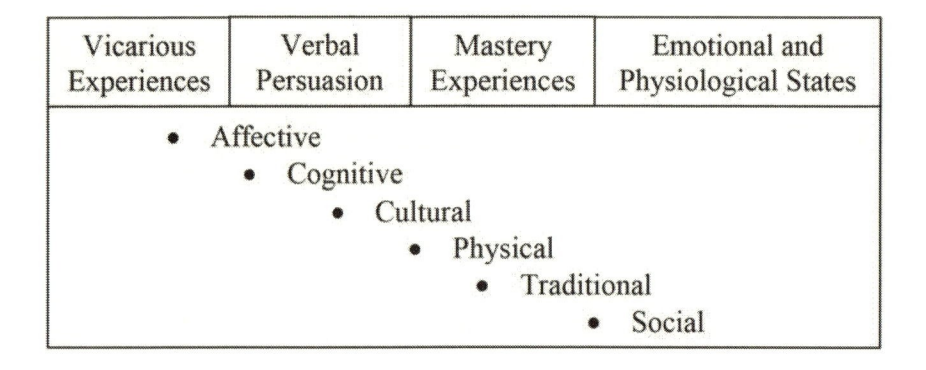

Figure 8.2. Lived Experiences Influence Understanding of and Actions Associated with Qualities Impacting Self-Efficacy and Integrity.

about themselves, with other people, and within society. Integrity is commonly described as doing the right thing, even when no one is watching.

PRINCIPLES OF MORALITY AND SOCIAL JUSTICE

Morality

Conversations related to ethics (external systems) and integrity (internal systems) must include the construct or principles of morality. Morality comprises the overarching standards and values acceptable within a society, usually framing the purposes and promises of an organization to society, accepted and adopted by each member. Frequently, morals are linked with virtues, i.e., characteristics valued as promoting both collective and individual good. Virtuous integrity or morality is about being good and becoming good (Curzer, 2012). Like integrity, virtues include, but are not limited to, traits of courage, temperance (self-control), liberality (generosity), magnificence (radiance), pride (self-satisfaction), honor (respect), good temper (equanimity), friendliness, truthfulness, wit, friendship (companionship), and justice (Rayner, 2011).

Morality in adults does not remain static; morality continues to change through life depending on many different factors (Noam, 1995). Members of societies are easily influenced by the voices heard and honored; all forms of media play significant roles in shaping societal morality. Judgments labeled as right or wrong can be affected directly and indirectly by various sources recently experienced and accumulated throughout life. Milner and Delale-O'Connor (2016) recommended that educators delve into all aspects of their own moral virtues, the origins of their moral understanding, the continuing influences on their moral development, and the manifestations of their morality. In particular, Milner and Delale-O'Connor (2016) advocated that educators examine the context of their virtues based on their cultural characteristics and their foundational rationalizations. If educators self-assess their own morals and analyze their purposes and priorities, they increase their awareness of the impact they make on their learners.

Social Justice

"Social justice in education is concerned with achieving equitable and quality education for all students" (Bell, 1997, p. 3). Social justice entails seeing and accepting ourselves and all other people for who the person is and where the person comes from as valuable (Belle, 2019) and equal participants in, contributors to, and recipients of recognition via time, attention, space, materials, actions, capacity, and, most importantly, voice and individuality.

Becoming aware of and being attentive to social justice also begins with an honest self-assessment; frequently educators have not conducted the depth of understanding necessary to reveal all beliefs and biases, especially a realistic examination of individual and affiliated group power and privilege. Understanding involves knowing all information from past and present, positive and negative, published and unpublished, and all perspectives. This process requires practicing critical thinking, withholding personal judgment, and contextualizing events relevant to local, national, and global history. With thorough knowledge and understanding, social justice educators are ready for tools for social change, advocacy, and activism (Hytten & Bettez, 2011).

Summary

People are drawn to becoming members of organizations and abiding by the ethics of the organization due to their individual integrity and virtues. However, the morality of a society is ever-changing, prompting modifications to organizational ethics and individual integrity. Figure 8.3 shows the overlapping influences of ethics and morality on Adrian's integrity and social justice as he grapples with authenticity of his course content, fairness of his class interactions, and usefulness of his comprehensive feedback for his online teaching and learning.

PRINCIPLES INTO PRACTICES

Ethical Standards

In the United States, most educators certified by the state and employed by K–12 school systems are cognizant of and compliant with their state department of education's code of ethics. These documents delineate the laws, purpose, definitions, expectations, disciplinary actions, and review schedules for updating the document.

In 1975, the National Education Association (NEA, n.d.) adopted their code of ethics for educators, focusing on two principles: (a) Principle I-Commitment to the Student and (b) Principle II-Commitment to the Profession. Each principle includes eight standards. In 1994, the Association of American Educators (AAE, n.d.) developed their code of ethics containing four basic principles: (a) Principle I-Ethical Conduct toward Students; (b) Principle II-Ethical Conduct toward Practices and Performance; (c) Principle III-Ethical Conduct toward Professional Colleagues; and (d) Principle IV-Ethical Conduct toward Parents and Community; each principle is detailed with multiple standards.

In 2015, the National Association of State Directors of Teacher Education and Certification [NASDTEC] published their Model Code of Ethics for

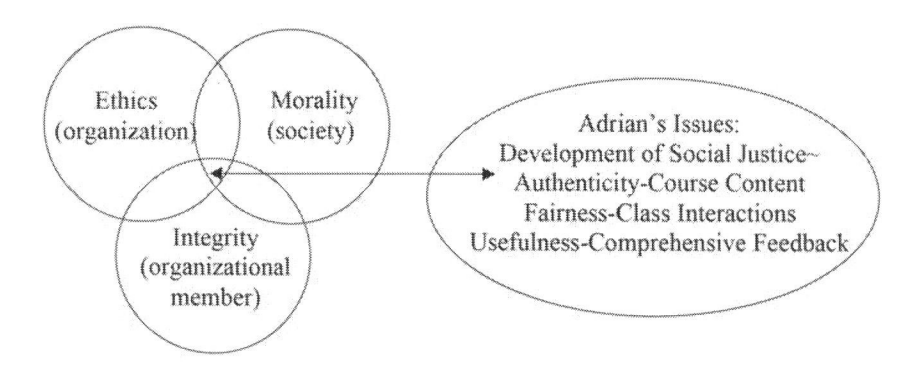

Figure 8.3. Ethics, Integrity, and Morality in Relationship to the Development of Social Justice associated with Adrian's Issues.

Educators [MCEE] (NASDTEC, 2015). This code features five principles: (a) Principle I-Responsibility to the Profession; (b) Principle II-Responsibility for Professional Competence; (c) Principle III-Responsibility to Students; (d) Principle IV-Responsibility to the School Community; and (e) Principle V-Responsible and Ethical Use of Technology. Again, each principle includes multiple standards and indicators detailing the expectations.

Teacher educators in higher education must comply with the expectations of their organizations, i.e., professional associations and faculty handbooks. Teacher educators are encouraged to become familiar with the Association of Teacher Educators (ATE, 2008), Standards for Teacher Educators that "describe how teacher educators impact the education of teachers: (para 1). Specifically, Standard 1, Teaching, emphasizes, "Modeling of behavior [that] relates to teaching, service, and scholarly productivity . . . [through the] use of research-based, proven best practices" (para 3).

Integrity Qualities

Integrity in teaching and learning promotes inquiry and knowledge development. For this process to be effective, an authentic commitment from the educator is required. Such a commitment can foster the idea of learning as a "mutual task" in which "the student may come to develop an inner confidence" so the learner can contribute to the learning experience (Nillsen, 2005, p. 89). During this process, the educator and learner go through a process of disequilibrium as their ideas are affirmed and challenged. While this process can seem like a chaotic situation, such a process is necessary for the promotion of intellectual integrity.

Intellectual integrity requires practices including respect, acceptance, care, compassion, honesty, fairness, trust, readiness, responsibility, selflessness, dedication, and so forth. Educators can ensure integrity by interacting sincerely with learners: greeting each learner to welcome them into their shared space, beginning each class session with a brief community meeting for learners to share social events, checking in with learners frequently during the learning experience to confirm understanding with the learners recapping information, asking open-ended questions allowing learners to make personal connections, and encouraging questioning both directly and indirectly related to content through guided practice.

Additionally, integrity in the classroom features: visiting with every learner during independent practice, facilitating closure for learners to share discoveries, conducting a meaningful post assessment to the learning experience, and ending each class by sharing personalized well wishes for every learning (Edgenuity, n.d.; Price-Mitchell, 2015; Simply Kinder, 2016).

Morality Guidelines

Most teacher educators rely primarily on their institutions of higher education faculty handbooks coupled with the morality of their professional organizations and society at large to frame their practices. In 2009, the American Association of University Professors [AAUP], (AAUP, 2009) published five principles, stated here in brief (The AAUP website provides detailed information.):

1. Professors, guided by a deep conviction of the worth and dignity of the advancement of knowledge, recognize the special responsibilities placed upon them. Their primary responsibility to their subject is to seek and to state the truth as they see it.
2. As teachers, professors encourage the free pursuit of learning in their learners. They hold before them the best scholarly and ethical standards of their discipline. Professors demonstrate respect for learners as individuals and adhere to their proper roles as intellectual guides and counselors.
3. As colleagues, professors have obligations that derive from common membership in the community of scholars. Professors do not discriminate against or harass colleagues.
4. As members of an academic institution, professors seek above all to be effective teachers and scholars. Although professors observe the stated regulations of the institution, provided the regulations do not contravene academic freedom, they maintain their right to criticize and seek revision.
5. As members of their community, professors have the rights and obligations of other citizens. Professors measure the urgency of these

obligations in the light of their responsibilities to their subject, to their learners, to their profession, and to their institution.

Albeit applicable to all professors in higher education, these five AAUP Principles on Professional Ethics help teacher educators in particular to balance their professional ethics, pedagogical integrity, personal morality, and social justice development in the context of their individual careers. As teacher educators enhance their own sense of self-efficacy and agency, they are introducing and practicing these theoretical frameworks with their teacher candidates.

Many teacher educators enter higher education with prior experiences as K–12 classroom teachers and/or school administrators. They bring a deep understanding of and thoughtful respect: for professional ethics as members of esteemed institutions of higher education; of the roles, readiness, and responsibilities of teacher educators; and the expectations of instructors of teacher education within their programs, departments, and colleges, expectations which are visible in their teaching, scholarship, service, and collegiality. Concomitantly, teacher educators tend to possess qualities of pedagogical integrity that communicate their credibility and commitment to all stakeholders directly and indirectly invested in education. Unfortunately, when teacher educators compromise their credibility and commitment to any of the stakeholders, their actions reflect on teacher education, the institution, and the individual teacher educator.

Teacher educators tend to experience comfort and competence that their professional ethics and pedagogical integrity are visible, viable, and valued in their face-to-face courses. Yet issues, such as Adrian's, arise with their online teaching and learning. Morality and social justice must also be considered.

Social Justice Development

All educators can develop the principles of social justice in themselves and their learners through mindful practices. Belle (2019) suggests the following strategies:

- Acknowledge everyone equally in the space/room using individual names. Avoid sharing favoritism or preferences for specific learners or guests.
- Know the learners in the space/room, i.e., know their affective, cultural, cognitive, economical, physical, traditional, and social characteristics, especially in relationship to the shared purposes for being together. Equally important, provide opportunities for all learners to know all other learners too.

- Share with your learners your own background, beliefs, behaviors, and yes, biases. In order for the group to grow in efficacy and agency, the teacher educator must provide appropriate role modeling.
- Plan activities, assignments, and assessments co-constructively *after* becoming acquainted with the learners yet *before* engaging in the plan. Start by identifying and agreeing upon the desired outcomes or end products. Then once all voices are heard, develop the plan with opportunities for each learner's greater strengths to be evident and each learner's lesser strengths to grow.
- Promote questioning by learners to delve into descriptions (what?), explanations (how?), justifications (why?), decision-makers (who?), alternatives (why not?). Learners must be encouraged to question the teacher educator, too.

Domingue (2016) offers the following pedagogical practices:

- Establish a community of learners through discussion postings and audio/visual connections, for example Facetime or Zoom.
- Design questioning to promote conversations eliciting multiple perspectives; activities can be introduced for various learners to be assigned explicit viewpoints that they must explain and defend.
- Feature course explorations on topics and issues of equality and inclusion related to the course purpose and educational goals.
- Customize at least one assignment that interrogates identities, i.e., investigate the learner's ethics, integrity, and morality in relationship to social justice in the classroom.
- Include closure to each learning experience that reinforces application of the concepts and practices in the context of social justice.

The following five aspects of course design are recommended based on the Berkeley University Center for Teaching and Learning (2020):

1. Foster Learners' Intrinsic Motivation. Accentuate the purpose of the course, relevance of the activities and assignments, use of learner-centered strategies, and connections with learners' lives and learning . . . present and future.
2. Emphasize Mastery Over Performance. Provide learners with choices in the ways they express their learning with their peers and with the instructor. Always equip learners with full instructions, all expectation criteria, and a comprehensive rubric with space for learners to self-assess their progress.
3. Conduct Frequent, Low-Stakes Assessments. Incorporating brief pre-assessments to start each learning experience, various types of forma-

tive assessments conducted directly and indirectly during the learning experience, and repeating the brief assessments as confirming post-assessments allow learners to comprehend and connect with the content and practices. Collect assignments as summative assessments throughout the course. When assessments are conducted frequently, teachers know their learners and can monitor their progress more easily; likewise, learners earn points gradually and can avoid the stress of the occasional, high-stakes assessment, usually administered as a test.
4. Build Learner Self-Efficacy. Provide opportunities for early success increase learner engagement, connections, and achievement. Teach developmentally appropriate learning strategies particularly helpful to the course content and practices. Relate course outcomes with applications to their lives.
5. Prepare Learners for Ethical Considerations in the Profession. Introduce the presence and power of ethics, integrity, and morality as learners in the course at an institution of higher education, as future professionals in their careers, and as members of society. Model the importance of ethics, integrity, and morality as their instructor.

However, like Adrian, when teacher educators are preparing and facilitating their online teaching and learning, they may grapple with issues of authenticity of the course content, fairness in the class interactions, and usefulness of the comprehensive feedback. Conducting quick visible checks of facial expressions, denoting learners' understanding, tend to become more difficult during online teaching and learning.

ETHICS, INTEGRITY, MORALITY, AND SOCIAL JUSTICE IN RELATIONSHIP TO ADRIAN'S ISSUES

Course Content

The content for a particular course in teacher education incorporates all of the knowledge, skills, and dispositions expected to be taught and learned, usually framed by the goals of a particular program. Ideally, the content, i.e., the concepts and practices, aligns with the instruction and the assessments, carefully assembled into one seamless, inclusive package. Developing course content requires teacher educators to use critical thinking and problem-solving to make endless decisions as they select or redirect every facet of the content, not only when preparing and facilitating the course for a particular semester, but also during the course in preparation for the next semester. Teacher educators must be constantly updating their own knowledge, skills, and dispositions to stay current in their academic areas: professionally and pedagogically.

A teacher educator's sense of ethics and integrity influences course content decisions and delivery in multiple ways. The teacher educator selects the books, articles, and websites that teacher candidates are expected to read and apply. These materials are grounded on various research, written from various perspectives, and communicate various messages that may or may not be accurate, neutral, and complete. Teacher educators must be attentive to possible subjectivity, bias, and partiality expressed in the content and selection of the readings. Such examination must attend to the ideas and voices that are "heard" within the materials as well as the voices that are "silenced" or "missing." If the teacher educator is seeking a particular agenda or angle related to a topic or issue for the candidates to experience, then the teacher educator should establish the purpose clearly. The teacher educator must ensure that a range of reading materials and resources is accessible by all learners and provides many different viewpoints.

Course content also includes the instruction and the assessments. Again, the teacher educator incorporates chosen methods to both facilitate and measure the learning in ways that are accurate, fair, equitable, and complete. Teacher educators must use many different instructional strategies that are meaningful, purposeful, and learner-centered.

Across the content, instruction, and assessments, teacher educators must allow learners choices. As the course unfolds, teacher educators should include learners in the co-construction of activities, assignments, and assessments; invite learners into the co-creation of instructional groups (so every learner interacts with every other learner in the class); and involve learners in choosing their individual connections with the content, assignments, and assessments. Teacher educators can preface opportunities for self-choice with instructions to choose a path to feature the learner's greater strength or to choose a path to focus on the learner's lesser strength.

Specific to online teaching and learning, teacher educators must determine when content will be made available, i.e., released to learners. Some teacher educators advocate preparing the whole course or at least a blueprint of the course in advance of the first session so learners can become acquainted with the material, schedule the due dates, and pace themselves appropriately. Some teacher educators release material as the course unfolds. Each teacher educator is encouraged to serve as a facilitator by polling their learners to ascertain the way a particular class wants materials released and then accommodating their preferences.

Teacher educators should share with the learners that no course can include all content relevant to the course. Nor can the content represent every perspective. Teacher educators should ask learners to post additional material and resources on the Discussion Board, as an assignment or for bonus points. Teacher educators can place learners in groups to debate the greater and lesser strengths of selected sources. Given that the learners in a teacher preparation course are learning to become educators, the teacher educator is always modeling thoughts, actions, and beliefs beneficial to the learners' college and career experience.

Class Interactions

Interactions within a particular class depend on the establishment of a community of learners where everyone feels like a visible, equal, respected, and included participant. Teacher educators must communicate and model a safe and welcoming community before the first class session through email, texts, and other university approved communication systems. Keeping Bandura's (1977) four sources of self-efficacy in mind, the teacher educator models and reinforces multisensory learning with every interaction (or absence of interaction). The teacher educator's integrity is quickly assessed by the learners when teacher educators' communications are timely, friendly (and appropriately humorous), respectful, clear, purposeful, productive, and succinct. Many communities of learners prefer weekly announcements as both a gentle reminder and supportive connection with the learners and teacher educator. Weekly reminders can offer additional information through links and attachments; however, weekly reminders should not include new activities, assignments, and/or assessments. If the teacher educator has discovered an error or needs to adjust material on the course website, then a separate announcement must be emailed centered on this singular item and the adjustment posted on the website. Additional time must be allocated for learners to accommodate the adjustments.

Information can be communicated orally during online teaching and learning through recorded and live presentations. When information is recorded, segments should be relatively short and focused on main ideas. Teacher educators are advised to record one segment conveying new content; record one or two different segments with activities, assignments, and assessments. When learners need to review the instructions, these different segments allow them to find the information more quickly.

During live presentations, teacher educators are urged to use a stack of 3 x 5 cards with each learner's name printed on the card. The teacher educator draws the name cards randomly to call on a learner to talk, i.e., share a connection, answer a question, and so on. During discussions, the teacher educator calls on every learner, asks various levels of questions and is aware of the random order so all learners are asked all levels of questions throughout the course, and allows time for every learner to respond. Teacher educators can use the name cards when grouping learners online for breakout conversations.

Comprehensive Feedback

Teacher preparation courses are offered for learners to acquire new concepts and practices in their roles as learners, to apply the concepts and practices to their repertoire in readiness for classrooms, and to advance their concepts and practices as K–12 classroom teachers with ethics and integrity. Comprehensive feedback from the teacher educator allows the learner to achieve these goals.

Comprehensive feedback includes four parts: (a) personalization, (b) accomplishments (evidence of greater strengths), (c) assistance (ways to improve lesser strengths to benefit the outcome), and (d) continuing support for motivation. Comprehensive feedback must focus on the expectations and outcome and not the learner.

Two important rules of ethics as associated directly with comprehensive feedback: (a) do no harm and (b) avoid score pollution. Do no harm (Payne, 2003) entails that the feedback is always kind, respectful, objective, positive, and professional in all communications. Teacher educators must consider the communication from the perspective of the recipient. Do no harm is easily understood and used by teacher educators; they recognize the influence of their feedback to promote engagement, connections, and achievement that will be used in the teacher candidates' own K–12 classrooms.

The rule of ethics to avoid score pollution (Haladyna et al., 1991; Popham, 1991) applies primarily to assessments (including activity checklists and assignment rubrics) and is more challenging for teacher educators. To avoid score pollution, teacher educators must score behaviors and submissions with no penalties added for items unrelated to learning the content. For example, pollutants include points for the learner's name and date on the submission; clarity of sentence, grammar, spelling; lateness of submission; and other items that may be included in the rubric but do not reflect learning the content. An appropriate approach would reduce the total number of possible points on the activities, assignments, and assessments to exclude these items, and add the corresponding percent to the final number of points possible for the course. Removing penalties points related to effort allows teacher educators to model developmentally appropriate practices for their learners to replicate in their own future classrooms.

ADRIAN'S GOALS

Teacher educators, like Adrian, rely upon their professional ethics and pedagogical integrity evident through their roles, readiness, and responsibility across their teaching, service, scholarship, and collegiality. Specifically, in his online teaching and learning, Adrian grapples with three issues: (a) authenticity of course content, (b) fairness of class interactions, and (c) usefulness of comprehensive feedback. He realizes that his thoughts, actions, and beliefs impact his learners as teacher candidates and as K–12 classroom teachers who, in turn, impact young learners. Adrian also acknowledges that he wants to lift himself to become the best teacher educator he can be, especially in his online teaching and learning.

To this end, Adrian sets five achievable goals related to his issues. For Goal 1, Adrian will prepare his course; invite a knowledgeable other, a colleague well-acquainted with classroom assessments, to carefully review the course; and ask the colleague for honest, detailed feedback. After he receives the feedback, he will modify his course content accordingly. For Goal 2, Adrian will invite another knowledgeable other, preferably a teacher, to carefully review the course content for application to contemporary K–12 classrooms.

For Goal 3, Adrian will invite his learners to complete quick electronic polls/surveys to provide him feedback. The surveys will delve into various aspects of course content, class interactions, and the comprehensive feedback. For Goals 4 and 5, Adrian will develop two different activities: one related to class interactions and one related to comprehensive feedback. Data analysis associated with these two activities will provide Adrian with additional insights for enhancing his efficacy and advancing his agency with deliberation, accountability, and virtue.

From the feedback, Adrian will become more aware and attentive to the presence and power of the principles of ethnics, integrity, morality, and social justice, not only in his online course, but also via the direct and indirect communication of the roles and responsibilities these principles play in the teaching and learning of all learners of all ages.

Reflection Questions

1. What are professional ethics?
2. How do you incorporate professional ethics into your content, interactions, and feedback as part of your teaching as a teacher educator?
3. How do you incorporate professional ethics into your content, interactions, and feedback as part of the learning for your learners as teacher candidates and as classroom teachers?
4. What is pedagogical integrity?
5. How do you incorporate pedagogical integrity into your content, interactions and feedback?
6. How do you incorporate pedagogical integrity into your content, interactions, and feedback as part of the learning for your learners as teacher candidates and as classroom teachers?
7. What is moral pedagogy?

8. How do you incorporate moral pedagogy into your content, interactions, and feedback?
9. What is social justice pedagogy?
10. How do you incorporate social justice pedagogy into your content, interactions, and feedback?

RESOURCES

Children's Library Lady. (2020). *Classroom resources for teaching integrity and principles.* https://childrenslibrarylady.com/teaching-integrity-principles/.
Keenan, J. F. (2015). *University ethics.* Rowman & Littlefield.
Mitchell, L. (2020). *6 strategies for successful distance learning. Edutopia.* https://www.edutopia.org/article/how-keep-students-attention-virtual-classroom.
Schulte, A. K. (2009). *Seeking integrity in teacher education.* Springer Publishing.
The George Washington University. (2020). *Guide of academic integrity in online learning environments* . https://studentconduct.gwu.edu/guide-academic-integrity-online-learning-environments.
UC San Diego. (2020). *Promoting academic integrity in digital learning.* https://digitallearning.ucsd.edu/whatwedo/integrity.html.

REFERENCES

American Association of University Professors [AAUP]. (2009). *Statement on professional ethics.* https://www.aaup.org/report/statement-professional-ethics.
Association of American Educators [AAE]. (n.d.). *Code of ethics for educators.* https://www.aaeteachers.org/index.php/about-us/aae-code-of-ethics.
Association of Teacher Educators [ATE]. (2008). *Standards for teacher educators* . https://www.ate1.org/standards-for-teacher-educators.
Bandura, A. (2000). Exercise of human agency through collective efficacy. *Current Directions in Psychological Science, 9*(3), 75–78.
Bandura A. (1977). Self-efficacy: Toward a unifying theory of behavioral change. *Psychological Review, 84* (2), 191–215.
Bandura, A. (2006). Toward a psychology of human agency. *Perspectives on Psychological Science, 1*(2), 164–180.
Bell, L. A. (1997). Theoretical foundations for social justice education. In M. Adams, L. A. Bell, & P. Griffin, (Eds.), *Teaching for diversity and social justice: A sourcebook* (pp. 3–15). Routledge.
Belle, C. (2019, Jan 23). What is social justice education anyway? *Education Week.* https://www.edweek.org/ew/articles/2019/01/23/what-is-social-justice-education-anyway.html.
Berkeley University Center for Teaching and Learning. (2020). *Academic integrity through course design.* https://teaching.berkeley.edu/resources/design/academic-integrity.
Curzer, H. J. (2012). Aristotle and the virtues. *Oxford Scholarship Online.* https://doi.org/10.1093/acprof:oso/9780199693726.001.0001.
Czimbal, B. & Brooks, M. (2006). Ethics & integrity. *Abundance Company.* https://www.abundancecompany.com/ethics_integrity.htm.
Domingue, A. D. (2016). Online and blended pedagogy in social justice education. In M. Adams & L. A. Bell, (Eds.) *Teaching for diversity and social justice* (pp. 369-396). Taylor & Francis Group.
Edgenuity. (n.d.). *Ensuring academic integrity in online learning.* https://www.edgenuity.com/academic-integrity-in-online-learning/.
Gallavan, N. P. (2002). Cultural competency for transformative education. In J. Wink and L. G. Putney, *Visions of Vygotsky* (pp. 157–175). Allyn and Bacon.

Haladyna, T. M., Nolen, S. B., & Haas, N. S. (1991). Raising standardized achievement test scores and the origins of test score pollution. *Educational Researcher, 20*(5), 2–7.

Hytten, K., & Bettez, S. C. (2011). Understanding education for social justice. *Educational Foundations, 25*(1), 7–24.

Indeed Career Guide. (2019, December 12). How to maintain professional integrity in the workplace. https://www.indeed.com/career-advice/career-development/maintaining-professional-integrity.

Jensen, M. C. (2009, September 16). Integrity, morality, and ethics. *Compliance Building*. https://www.compliancebuilding.com/2010/09/16/integrity-morality-and-ethics/.

Juneja, P. (2015). The importance of ethics. *Management Study Guide*. https://www.managementstudyguide.com/importance-of-ethics.htm.

Milner, H. R. IV, & Delale-O'Connor, L. (2016). Toward (whose) morality in teacher education. *Action in Teacher Education, 38*(3), 217–220.

Mintz, S. (2017, March 28). Why do we need ethics? *The Ethics Sage*. https://www.ethicssage.com/2017/03/why-do-we-need-ethics.html.

National Association of State Directors of Teacher Education and Certification [NASDTEC]. (2015). Model Code of Ethics for Educators [MCEE]. https://www.nasdtec.net/page/MCEE_Doc.

National Education Association [NEA]. (n.d.) Code of Ethics http://www.nea.org/home/30442.htm.

Nillsen, R. (2005). The concept of integrity in teaching and learning. *Journal of University Teaching and Learning Practice, 2*(3), 85–93.

Noam, G. (1995). Reconceptualizing maturity: The search for deeper meaning. In G. G. Noam & K. W. Fischer (Eds.), *Development and vulnerability in close relationships*. Erlbaum.

Payne, D. A. (2003). *Applied educational assessment* (2nd ed.). Wadsworth Publishing.

Popham, W. J. (1991). Appropriateness of teachers' test preparation practices. *Educational Measurement: Issues and Practice, 10*(4), 12–15.

Price-Mitchell, M. (2015, September 8). Integrity in the classroom: How K–12 teachers influence tomorrow's ethical leaders. *Psychology Today*. https://www.psychologytoday.com/us/blog/the-moment-youth/201509/integrity-in-the-classroom.

Rayner, V. (2011, June 12). 12 virtues introduced by Aristotle: The master of those who know. https://aesthetichealingmindset.wordpress.com/2011/06/12/4706/.

Simply Kinder. (2016, August). Teaching with integrity; Simple ways you can change your mindset to have a successful school year. https://www.simplykinder.com/teaching-with-integrity/.

Chapter Nine

Efficacy and Agency

Walter S. Polka and Amanda Rudolph

Efficacy and agency become intertwined in our personal and professional lives as we navigate changes in our contexts and expectations over time. They both become integral parts of our continuously evolving educator identity. For this chapter, both efficacy and agency are discussed, with individual vignettes to begin and conclude the chapter that synthesize the significance of both qualities applicable to online teaching and learning for teacher educators.

EFFICACY VIGNETTE

William Stephen Peterman graduated with a Bachelor of Arts degree in history from a major northeast public university. During his undergraduate studies he did not take any education courses. After completing his degree requirements, William enrolled in a private university for his Master of Arts degree in history. He was unsure if he wanted to continue in the tourist management business in which he had worked throughout college. He decided to take an elective History of Education course and began a year of substitute teaching. Thus, William's teaching career began as a per diem substitute teacher. He enjoyed the various classroom settings where he substituted and often reflected about his diverse learning experiences and effective student interactions. As a result, William was convinced that education was definitely the most appropriate career option for him.

With time, experience, and perseverance, William built upon his personal self-efficacy to develop his professional self-efficacy, earned multiple graduate degrees and achieved success as an effective classroom teacher, school administer, and teacher educator. Throughout his career, William posited that, "Without classroom interactions, learning would be limited and the 'high-touch' caring approach would become lost to 'high-tech' programmed expectations." However, the day arrived that William was asked to move his courses online. Since that day, William's various online courses continue to reflect his "high-touch" teaching orientation and he still contends that, "My insistence on making my online classes as similar to my previous 'face-to-face' experiences in terms of class activities and teaching strategies has facilitated my transition from a pre-digital age, but very good classroom teacher, to an excellent digital age online professor."

Efficacy Discussion

William definitely made a successful transition to digital age online teaching and learning. He admits it wasn't always easy, due primarily to unpredictable technical glitches, but the technology is much better and more reliable now than in the past. He avers, "Teachers just have to learn to 'go with the flow' of contemporary times just like they expect their students to do." Indeed, instructors need to find ways to effectively adapt the activities they always liked facilitating in face-to-face classrooms to the online platforms of their respective institutions. Educators must continue to creatively experiment with technology and appreciate that online experiences present greater opportunities for differentiation of instruction.

Bandura (1977, 1986, 1997) defines personal efficacy as the belief in one's own ability to succeed at accomplishing desired levels of performance. An individual with a strong sense of efficacy demonstrated spontaneous creativity and an unbridled commitment to succeed when faced with challenges. Efficacious individuals enjoy challenges because they summarily believe that they can control most of the various components associated with any situation and, in the end, truly feel good about their creative ability in overcoming the obstacles presented. They possess an optimistic attitude about themselves and demonstrate an authentic caring disposition to the people, things, and ideas that confront them.

William's educational career history pragmatically illustrates his personal and professional efficacy. As an uncertified, and basically an "unschooled," beginning, per diem substitute teacher, he accepted the *challenge* of the diverse classroom contexts he faced on a daily basis without pedagogical training and supervision and was able to not only survive but also thrive. He demonstrated a strong *commitment* to teaching and learning based on his desire to improve classroom experiences for all students. He was acutely aware of the intervening factors that he could *control* in various classroom settings and he developed the ability to effectively manage them. He generally *cared* about the students and the subject matter they were to learn and he *creatively* applied his unique interpersonal style, sense of humor, and "high-touch" approach in implementing lessons.

William's efficacy manifestations are based on those five above mindset dispositions associated with positively coping with personal and professional changes, as reinforced by various researchers: *challenge, commitment, control, creativity,* and *caring* (Beirne, 2006; Brockbank et al., 2017; Csikszentmihalyi, 1990; DePree, 1989; Hall, & Hord, 2006; Illeris, 2018; Kobasa et al., 1982; Pieters, 2017; Polka, 2007, 2010; Polka et al., 2014; Polka et al., 2017; Silva & Coelho, 2019; Stossell, 1992). Those dispositions enabled William to succeed in different educational situations including his current online teaching.

William adroitly adapted to the various educational dynamics that he encountered during his career. He worked compassionately to:

- meet the needs and interests of various unique people (i.e., preK–16 students, graduate students, parents, colleagues, administrators, board of education members or community advocates);
- manage constantly changing educational things (i.e., classroom configurations, budget issues, technology, supplies, and materials); as well as to
- continuously interact with evolving ideas associated with learning and teaching (i.e., inclusion, diversity, discipline approaches, differentiation of instruction).

As his story illustrates he was successful in preK–12 classrooms as a substitute or regular teacher; in districtwide administration as a curriculum and instructional leader or as superintendent of schools, and in higher education as a professor of advanced graduate students.

So what does William specifically do today as a successful online teacher in his synchronous online courses that he recommends other professionals consider? These examples demonstrate the adaptations that he contends efficacious online instructors employ in online courses based on those five enumerated personal mindset dispositions:

1. ***Challenge***: Recognize that technology, like people and ideas, will constantly change. Online technology has become more efficient and more user-friendly than previously. The inclusion of live video streaming encourages student interactions, so build in multiple student interactive experiences. Divide students into primary and secondary groups and jigsaw them in online conference rooms to complete cooperative learning activities. However, expect that technological glitches may occur and always have "backup" plans of action.
2. ***Commitment***: Be sure that students appreciate the incredible opportunities that online education presents for them in terms of learning

efficiency and their own self-efficacy. Students can participate in learning experiences in various ways and can learn in any place at their convenience. Students have more control over their learning experiences than ever before. And, as the instructor, it is imperative to recognize the professional freedom and flexibility that you now possess. Students may be engaged online at the teacher's convenience from any site including: home, hotel rooms, airport lounges, actually anywhere in the world but be sure your internet connections work effectively. Maintain your positive attitude to this "high-tech" approach to learning as a viable option in our contemporary world but keep focused on the "high-touch" aspect of teaching and learning.

3. ***Control***: Appreciate the elements of online learning that you can control and don't become too stressed about those that you can't control. You can control the general conference interactions between you and the students by appropriately using the "mute" button and other built-in program features such as "show of hands" to focus discussions and reduce unnecessary chatter. Remember that online instructors even control when and where they park their automobiles! But do note that you can't control the weather and "power-outages" may occur so be prepared.

4. ***Creativity***: Continue to "think outside the box" as you would in regular classrooms and design online lessons that reflect and enable creativity for you and your students to complete assignments. Provide students with opportunities to "Post" their essays, reflections, and other assignments on course "Discussion Boards" to encourage "critical friend" evaluative responses to each other's work. The posting of assignments and reflections has a positive impact on the quality of submissions as now students can review each other's work and recognize that their assignment submissions are "public" to everyone in the course. Also, be sure to empower students to consider alternatives to course assignments based on their interests, needs, and learning styles.

5. ***Caring***: Students at all levels of the instructional spectrum, pre-K to doctoral, truly don't care how much the teacher knows until they know how much the teacher cares about them and their colleagues. Establish opportunities for everyone in the course, including the instructors, to "get to know each other personally" prior to the start of the first online session. A digital portfolio is a good tool to have students present personal and professional information about themselves as well as to respond to the posted digital portfolios of others to determine "connections" between them. Digital portfolios can be completed in a variety of formats (PowerPoints presentations, Prezi, renderforest, livebinders, designshare, etc.) using sound and movie clips as well as photos to highlight significant life events and individual specific inter-

ests. Online instructors also must share information about themselves using their respective digital portfolio to model the experience and present their "high-touch" personal side to students. Also, encourage a "family friendly" attitude for online sessions and recognize the "high-touch" personal value to individuals when they have their spouses, children, or pets "drop in" to online conferences to say, "Hello, or Goodnight"!

The following email (personal correspondence, 01/29/20) from one of Dr. Peterman's current graduate students summarizes the value of the above recommendations as well as the essence of his successful replication of effective pre-digital classroom approaches to contemporary operative online courses based on blending "high-touch" teaching with "high-tech" learning:

Hi Dr. P!
I thoroughly enjoyed this evening; it was a new experience for me and I felt like I was sitting in a physical classroom. . . . Thank you so much for your humor and for sharing your wisdom with us on this evening. Your facilitation was thought provoking, and I am excited to learn and grow with you. You made me feel like a part of the family, and I really appreciate that. My transition was smooth, and stress free which was a super relief for me. I will upload my digital portfolio shortly, and will view some of the portfolios of my peers way before the next class. Until then, be safe, and enjoy the rest of the week. Thanks,
Kenyah Koonce-Miller, Instructional Coach for K–5 Mathematics;
Merrick Academy, Queens Public Charter School, District 29
Queens, New York City, NY (personal correspondence)

AGENCY VIGNETTE

Sally was in her second year as an assistant professor when she learned she would be taking over the one online course in the department. Immediately, she emailed her colleagues who had taught the class in prior years. These professors, both of whom where retiring, had created this course as one of the first online courses at their university. Luckily, both were willing to meet with her. Sally really needed some guidance; she hadn't even seen the course. The first professor, Frank, shared with Sally that the course really teaches itself, i.e., quizzes on the teaching standards are taken to prepare candidates for their tests, and review activities are provided to help them. Additionally, by reading the instruction, candidates construct their teacher work samples.

The second professor, Jodi, emphasized that the four face-to-face meetings are the most important part of the course. Understanding that the course is completely online, Sally realized that Jodi expected candidates to participate in ways that were not in the syllabus.

Experiencing much confusion, Sally contacted the university Office of Instructional Technology where she found courses to guide and support her with her sense of agency or ownership applicable to online teaching and learning. Sally was motivated to ask questions, learn new information, and, most importantly, incorporate innovations into her course.

Agency Discussion

According to Bandura (2001), agency is the ability to effect change in oneself, adapt, and renew. Then teacher agency can be considered the ability of teachers to affect change in their professional growth. Teachers may utilize professional development, professional collaboration, or self-reflection to create change in their practice. Throughout a professional career a teacher may face pedagogical and instructional changes that must be addressed through agency. Nowhere is this more important than in the online teaching movement of today.

As a teacher moving to an online environment, one's teaching methods may not translate exactly to the new medium. As discussed throughout this book, online teaching has unique challenges. Teachers in face-to-face classrooms may not quickly adapt to the new environment. Compared to face-to-face classroom teachers, online instructors may face isolation by the hours spent in front of the computer creating content and communicating with students. They may feel frustrated as face-to-face classroom teaching methods prove difficult to implement in the online environment. But even as these challenges arise, opportunities that were not available in the face-to-face classroom environment also open up.

Just as a new teacher begins to achieve efficacy and agency, a new online teacher begins the same process. Bandura (2001) articulates the four components of human agency: intentionality, forethought, self-reactiveness, and self-reflectiveness. Each one moves the teacher forward in their professional development. Sally is a good example of this process.

Intentionality

When considered in relation to teachers, intentionality can be considered the plan of action teachers take to grow. To better effect the success of their students, teachers need to be deliberate about their professional development. Think back to the example, Sally began by seeking out mentors and veteran online teachers. As teachers think about online pedagogy it is not enough to rely on traditional professional development or even prior learning to acclimate to efficacy in the online platform, teachers need to think of new resources and research for growth.

Forethought

This second component of agency requires the intentionality to also have direction. Not only do teachers begin to work toward agency by creating a plan of action, they also need to be thoughtful in creating that plan. Consideration is given to a direction in the professional development and growth needed. In the example of Sally, she identified a lack of experience in teaching in an online environment and then set out a deliberate path to gain some professional development.

Self-reactiveness

One of the major challenges of teaching and teaching online is time management. In today's world, time is always short. Time can also be a challenge to plan and complete any professional development or training to gain skills needed to be successful in the classroom. Self-reactiveness is the ability to motivate and follow through with planned professional growth. In the previous scenario, Sally sought out veteran professors and their opinions and then followed the advice of her chair to visit the Office of Instructional Technology for professional development. In her case, the university had created many professional development opportunities for faculty members to learn about learning management systems, video conferencing, and other online teaching strategies. To become a successful teacher, Sally motivates herself to attend and seek out trainings and workshops.

Self-reflection

The final component of teacher agency is self-reflection. Evaluating the experiences of professional development and growth may be the most overlooked component of teacher agency. Just as preservice teachers are encouraged to reflect and journal about their practice, online teachers need to also take the time to think about practice and their growth. Through self-reflection, online teachers can identify their successes and areas that still need growth.

Therefore, teachers may be challenged to grow as they face online teaching for the first time. What is critical to good practice is that teachers use their agency to seek out, attend, and learn from new professional opportunities. By being deliberate and reflective, teachers can formulate a successful plan to grow as an online educator just like Sally.

ROLES FOR INSTRUCTORS TO ENHANCE EFFICACY AND AGENCY

Effective instructors benefit by considering twelve important roles to fulfill that enhance both their efficacy and agency. Applicable to all instruction, too often these roles are fulfilled naturally during face-to-face instruction. For some instructors, the roles will occur more naturally; for some instructors, the role must be incorporated intentionally. For all instructors, these roles offer insight and inspiration to provide more fulfilling learning experiences and academic outcomes for students.

1. **City Planner**—City planners design ways to optimize the city's land and resources in accordance to the governing laws and residents' preferences. As you design your course, consider ways to optimize the online platform and link resources in accordance with state, university, and program regulations coupled with the participants' preferences. Start with the home page for clear, easy-to-find-and-follow instructions. Carefully design each module so the curriculum, instructions, and assessments not only align with one another, but also offer consistency throughout the course. Label headings and subheadings using the same coding systems and writing patterns. Likewise, title links and attachments in ways that the titles connect with particular modules and in a logical sequence. Construct rubrics with detailed criteria that match the instructions, allowing space for self-assessment and instructor assessment; provide feedback that is timely, individualized, objective, specific, and encouraging. The purpose is to provide opportunities for growth based on positive, productive, and professional assessment and feedback. After you have prepared your feedback, ask yourself if the feedback would help you to achieve the goals if you were the recipient.
2. **Store Greeter**—Everyone participating in the course wants to feel safe, welcome, wanted; to have a sense of belonging. For online courses, the home page serves as an attractive welcome mat extending friendly greetings and helpful information in easy-to-find-and-understand language. Likewise, all correspondence—announcements, email, and so on—must communicate an authentic appreciation for participating and supportive clarification addressing questions, concerns, suggestions.
3. **Tour Guide**—Noticeably evident on the home page must be the instructions, or the map of the web site, orienting students in their navigation to the various features and functions. Some academic institutions expect instructors to use similar web site templates, reducing time spent by students finding the features and functions. To ensure

that your web site is easily navigable, ask two friends (one colleague and one not a colleague) to tour your web site and give you honest feedback.
4. **Learning Facilitator**—Shift your self-view of instructor from course deliverer to learning facilitator. Your goal is to equip and empower your students with the knowledge, skills, and dispositions framing the course so they are ready for their next steps (academic competence, self-confidence, critical thinking, advanced courses, new profession, leadership roles, etc.). When your students experience confusion or challenges, reflect on and inspect carefully your content and practices. Efficacy and agency mean you are responsible for making the learning more meaningful and memorable; therefore, you must modify your content and practices to ensure clarity, comprehension, and connections.
5. **Instructional Coach**—As a facilitator, you also become an instructional coach. Listen attentively and read closely, consider communicated information for purpose and from multiple perspectives, express appreciation for the contact, and provide appropriate information. Although you may be inclined to capture the teachable moment and share a great amount of information, you may discover that short, constructive, and immediate responses are better. However, in all situations, check in again with the student to guarantee that your feedback was useful.
6. **Engine Mechanic**—When our vehicles release unrecognizable sounds or operate uncooperatively (or perhaps do not operate at all), we analyze the situation and make the necessary repairs so the vehicle functions safely, confidently, and comfortably. Online courses require engine mechanics to be aware of the content, practices, and assignments, i.e., the vehicle, posted online as well as the safety, confidence, and comfort of the students, i.e., the drivers of the vehicle. Just as drivers of vehicles who prefer various features and routines, students prefer various features and routines.
7. **Motivational Speaker**—All students benefit from encouragement and humor. Students also appreciate knowing you as a person as well as a professional, and, most importantly, as a human who has real-world experiences, has made mistakes, and is vulnerable. Coupled with instructional coaching, your role as motivational speaker allows students to develop profound, perhaps, life-changing, learning experiences.
8. **Camera Operator**—Frequently when we order items online, the vendor provides views from all angles so we are well acquainted with the product. Similarly, television shows and movies use recording mechanisms that allow the viewer to experience the scene from multiple

perspectives. Think of your online teaching and learning as a camera operator. You will benefit by viewing your content, practices, and expectations through every possible angle prior to releasing these items to your students. Be aware that your students are becoming familiar with you, the format, their peers, and all the new information. They bring an unlimited range of prior knowledge and experiences associated with their personal growth, professional development, and pedagogical advancement. As you learn about your students, be ready to modify your camera settings to accommodate their affective, cultural, cognitive, economic, physical, traditional, and social characteristics.

9. **Party Host**—Without intentional efforts to build a positive social environment, online learning can feel lonely and impersonal. As a result, the online teacher must serve like a great party host, facilitating introductions, using discussion starters to facilitate conversations among students, and taking the time necessary to get to know students and reference new knowledge, skills, and dispositions via meaningful interactions with students as group members and as individuals.

10. **Lifeguard**—Online courses offer pools of content and sometimes students can get in over their heads with the concepts, practices, and expectations. The teacher is a kind of lifeguard who intentionally allows learners to wade or swim through all depths and breadths of water in ways that are developmentally appropriate for students and their learning. Sometimes instructors allow learners to wade or swim in the content one week at a time. Other times, instructors allow students to swim in particular parts of the content at a time or enjoy an open swim.

11. **Secret Sleuth**—Everything is documented in an online course. The teacher can tell when and how many times a student logs into the course, what pages were viewed or not viewed, how many discussions posts the student contributed, and much more. These data can be used to make adjustments and informed decisions as the instructor. If a student is not logging in, then the instructor should contact the student. If a student is not visiting modules with key instructions in a timely manner, instructors should contact the individual students to inquire about their situations, offer assistance, and discuss their progress.

12. **Lifelong Learner**—Great teachers are lifelong learners, and they can model that learning for their students in a variety of ways in the online classroom. The instructor can be an active (but not too active or it will silence students) participant in online discussions, sharing what they are learning about the subject, and even complete all or parts of some assignments, sharing their work with the students. This modeling is

effective in establishing a vibrant and dynamic online learning community where every student also becomes a lifelong learner.

RESILIENCY

Understanding and enhancing a person's efficacy and agency, especially with online teaching and learning, benefits significantly when instructors are aware of and maintain their resiliency, i.e., abilities to function without being overwhelmed or acting in dysfunctional or destructive ways; abilities to recover quickly from accidents and adversity. Instructors are encouraged to delve into their inner direction and self-motivation; investigate their perceptiveness, perseverance, and positivity; connect with communities, avenues of creativity, and love of learning; and notice their sense of spirituality, humor, flexibility, and self-worth. The qualities of efficacy, agency, and resiliency rely upon an instructor's honesty reflection and authentic commitment to build upon their greater strengths to fortify their lesser strengths.

REFLECTION QUESTIONS

1. How do the five Cs contribute to growth in personal and professional self-efficacy?
2. Does self-efficacy of online teaching and learning develop differently than face-to-face teaching and learning?
3. What are ways to encourage teacher educators and classroom teachers to create and implement professional development plans for themselves? Why is encouragement important?
4. Why is teacher agency important to online teaching? How do you think agency will affect the future of online teaching and learning?

RESOURCES

- Utilize your learning management system. Many LMS have built in training for users.
- Online Learning Consortium—This professional group offers a variety of resources about online teaching. Visit the website at https://onlinelearningconsortium.org/.
- National Education Association's Guide to Teaching Online course can be downloaded at http://www.nea.org/home/30103.htm.
- US Distance Learning Association—This professional organization offers many resources including a certification. Visit the website at https://usdla.org/.

REFERENCES

Bandura, A. (1977). Self-efficacy: Toward a unifying theory of behavioral change. *Psychology Review, 84*(2), 191–215.

Bandura, A. (1986). *Social foundations of thought and action*. Prentice-Hall.

Bandura, A. (1997). *Self-efficacy: The exercise of control*. Freeman.

Bandura, A. (2001). Social cognitive theory: An agentic perspective. *Annual Review of Psychology, 52,* 1–26.

Beirne, M. (2006). *Empowerment and innovation: Managers, principles and reflective practice*. Edward Elgar Publishing.

Brockbank, A., McGill, I., & Beech, N. (2017). Reflective learning in practice. In A. Brockbank, I. McGill, & N. Beech (Eds.), *Reflective learning in practice* (pp. 18–28). Gower Publishing Co.

Csikszentmihalyi, M. (1990). *Flow*. Harper & Row.

DePree, M. (1989). *Leadership is an art*. Dell.

Hall, G., & Hord, S. (2006). *Implementing change: Patterns, principles and potholes* (2nd ed.). Allyn & Bacon.

Illeris, K. (2018). A comprehensive understanding of human learning. In K. Illeris (Ed.), *Contemporary theories of learning* (pp. 1–14). Routledge.

Kobasa, S., Maddi, T. & Kahn, S. (1982). Hardiness and health: A prospective study. *Journal of Personality and Social Psychology, 42*(1), 168–177.

Pieters, G. (2017). *The ever-changing organization: Creating the capacity for continuous change, learning, and improvement*. St. Lucie Press.

Polka, W. (2007). Managing people, things and ideas in the 'effective change zone': A high-touch approach to educational leadership at the dawn of the twenty-first century. *Educational Planning, 16*(1), 12–17.

Polka, W. (2010). The art and science of constructivist supervision: Transforming schools by applying needs-based research. *Journal for the Practical Application of Constructivist Theory in Education, 5*(1), 1–28.

Polka, W., Wolfgang, J., & Mete, R. (2017). Serendipitous educational planning: Expeditiously applying Effective Change Zone (ECZ) mindset concepts. *Educational Planning. 24*(3), 25–44.

Polka, W., Wolfgang, J., Mete, R., Ayaga, A., & Khokhar, A. (2014). Planning to effectively motivate digital-age learners by addressing their "high-tech" interests and their "high-touch" needs. *Educational Planning, 21*(4). 51–68.

Silva, D., & Coelho, A. (2019). The impact of emotional intelligence on creativity, the mediating role of worker attitudes and the moderating effects of individual success. *Journal of Management & Organization, 25*(2), 284–302.

Stossell, J. (1992). *ABC 20/20 report on the mystery of happiness: Who has it . . . and how to get it*. American Broadcasting Company.

Chapter Ten

Stories from the Field

Lori Fulton, Jon Yoshioka, John Hicks,
Glenda L. Black, Rosela C. Balinbin Santos,
Mark M. Diacopoulous, V. Carole Smith,
and Erin O. Shaw

So . . . What now?

You started out learning how *Inspirations and Aspirations* are essential in setting the foundation for both teacher and teacher candidate success. Then how *Cultural Competence and Global Awareness* can be seamlessly integrated into the *Content, Pedagogical, and Andragogical Knowledge, Skills, and Dispositions* that all educators need to be successful. Being able to tailor *Classroom Assessment and Meaningful Feedback* to one's candidates' needs then became the goal as we created the *Collaborative Learning Communities* that allowed candidates to fully experience the benefits of online education. Finally, once the foundation was set for an engaging, rewarding experience, the inclusion of *Professional Integrity and Ethics* allowed us to help our candidates act with a sense of *Efficacy and Agency* in their interactions with all of their educational community members.

How does all of this apply to what we do on a daily basis?

To get the answer to this and other questions you may have, the best solution is to go directly to *Stories from the Field* where colleagues tell you, in their own words, how the process of teaching and learning online worked for them. The stories begin with Glenda's story, where she shares her experience as a learner in an online course. Then this chapter moves to John's and Rosela's stories from the perspectives of the instructors and how they struggled then successfully transitioned from face-to-face courses to online courses over time.

That was going to be the end of things. But right as we were getting ready to publish this book, the world as we knew it changed. Significantly. And we, as teachers, needed to find ways to navigate the new challenges before us. Fortunately, some of our colleagues had stories to tell around this transition as well.

This chapter now also includes stories from those who were thrust into online teaching due to the COVID-19 pandemic. The COVID stories begin with Mark's perspective as a beginning teacher educator and then V. Carole's perspective as a field supervisor and how she supported teacher candidates as they finished their education and prepared to begin their careers in education. Finally, Erin shares her perspective as a media specialist supporting educators as they moved their teaching online.

GLENDA'S STORY – THE THREE AMIGAS

Twenty years ago, I was a classroom teacher with three young children. I had just completed my master's of education degree and wanted to pursue a doctorate, but I was reluctant to continue my educational aspirations because of the time-consuming commute required to attend face-to-face classes on campus. My husband and I were already sharing chauffeuring duties for our children's sports, dance, music, and other activities. And was I not willing to put my career or family life on hold to attend the required face-to-face year of residency.

Then, an option appeared—I found out about universities starting to offer online graduate courses. Although I had never taken an online class before, this sounded like the perfect solution and I decided to apply to a doctoral program at a university that offered their courses online. With the exception of three flexible timed on-campus residencies, this program delivered completely asynchronous classes. My colleagues and my own research cautioned me that online learning was an isolated, independent, and impersonal experience, yet it felt right.

Like all other graduate students, time was always a challenge. For me, entering the virtual classroom required more engagement with the content, other learners, and written expression than I had ever experienced in a brick-and-mortar classroom. Sitting quietly in the back of the classroom was not an option—participation was required . . . for grades. However, there were unexpected positive outcomes from my online learning. I learned that adding humor and metaphors to explain my thinking was a strength. I also learned that I was not alone on this doctoral journey. A virtual sense of community was developed that evolved into a friendship that has lasted almost fifteen years.

Although Caroline*, Emma*, (pseudonyms) and I started the doctoral program at the same time, we were not always in the same courses or attended the same residencies. Instructors used a range of strategies to build community, which included consistent communication and feedback, they encouraged sharing personal and professional updates, and assigned collaborative work to achieve learning goals. In the first course, we were assigned to work together on an assignment. As Caroline, Emma, and I progressed in the program, instructors allowed students to share their preferences for who they wanted to work with on team assignments. Assignment conversations led to communicating through the courses providing each of us with personal and program support.

Caroline, Emma, and I were concerned our friendship would fade in time when we finished our degrees. We decided that when we finished the program we would meet once a year for a weekend in a different city. We have met annually for twelve years in New York, Boston, Toronto, Philadelphia, Vegas, Quebec City, Charlotte, Chicago, Cincinnati, Niagara Falls, Washington, and St. Louis. As online learners, we call ourselves The Three Amigas. Each amiga has used her experience as an online student to build community in her own online classes.

P.S. The Three Amigas are planning their next annual weekend.

JOHN'S STORY—LEARNING TO TEACH ONLINE: FACILITATING COMMUNITY AND PERSONAL INFLUENCE IN AN ONLINE ENVIRONMENT

Truth be told, I didn't want any part of teaching online seven years ago when I had been forced to take a very popular face-to-face course that featured a lot of hands-on learning experiences and put it online. I balked at the request, but realizing I really didn't have a choice, like many of you, I reluctantly complied. And it did not go well.

I had begun teaching high school English in the late 1980s, and my classes were always marked by high energy and engagement. I pride myself on the "personal influence" I had with my students in face-to-face settings. I did not believe I could cultivate a "living presence" that was immediately responsive to my teacher candidates in an online format even with more sophisticated technology being developed. All my strengths seemed limited, even diminished, and my belief that successful teaching must be a lived community between teacher and candidates seemed impossible. I was an "analogue man" living in a digital world.

My candidates suffered while I continued to offer underwhelming instruction in this course for two full academic years. Then, four years ago, in the summer, I was assigned to teach two shorter, month-long sessions of the course. The candidates in one of the sections prompted a dispositional change in me. Two candidates were twin brothers who both taught high school math in the same building. They were also a couple of real characters who energized our online class discussions with their great wit.

The experiences in this course caused me to loosen up and share a bit more of the self I had always shared so easily in my face-to-face courses. The twins' engaging demeanors caught on with all of us, and it prompted the candidates to ask me for real-time, synchronous chats, which I had not used up until then.

The class also prompted me to post an online photo of myself for the first time. Candidates had all posted photos of themselves and they felt it only right that I do the same. They even specified that I shouldn't post a "fake" school photo but something more casual and "real" as they had all done. So, I posted a photo of me watching a football game decked out in sweatshirt and hat. It was a hit. It humanized me.

Feeling energized by this great bunch of summer teacher candidates, I made even more additions to the fall semester version of the course. The first thing I added was an interest inventory. I don't know why I hadn't done this before because in my face-to-face classes, I had always spent the majority of the first two weeks getting to know my candidates. This opportunity was a hit. The candidates began sharing all kinds of things with me and their peers and it helped build that sense of community.

I also began to use audio recordings of my feedback on their work, which I could tell by their reactions, allowed that "personal influence" to operate in the online setting much as it had in my traditional classrooms. Over our winter break, I was pleased to learn that the opinions of my online candidates were now becoming very favorable with regard to my efforts. One candidate's comment, in particular, stood out to me. The candidate wrote, "Loved the professor's attitude in this class . . . I felt like he was really 'with me' the entire way!"

Emboldened by this positive feedback, I continued to find ways to make my online courses more like my high energy on-campus courses despite the trouble in finding opportunities for synchronous activities. While I kept traditional objective testing, I expanded my assessment choices and offered alternative or authentic forms of assessment, much as I had always done in my traditional classrooms. The student evaluations for my courses in the spring were even more favorable than those of the past fall and I also noticed a much higher percentage of the candidates were taking the time to complete them even though they were not mandatory. They expressed gratitude for being able to choose different ways to respond to the material. I knew I was finally reaching them and giving them a worthwhile learning experience. This fantastic feedback was confirmed, interestingly enough, in several face-to-face encounters over the next two years.

The first, and most dramatic encounter, occurred at a pool party at my best friend's house where over 100 people often gathered at his summer pool parties. As I arrived at the first party of the summer, I saw my friend's wife standing near the pool. She was pointing at me and saying, "He's here, he's here" to someone who was in the swimming pool. Then a woman I didn't recognize leaped out of the pool, ran up, hugged me, and identified herself as being one of the teacher candidates in my online class that spring. "I feel like I know you so well from the class," she said. I realized I did really know her well from the efforts I had made to create a real online community.

The next spring, a young woman waiting on me and some friends at a local pub recognized me because I was wearing the same baseball hat as in my online photo in the course she had taken with me the past fall. After praising me for what she thought was a very valuable online experience, she took our orders. As she brought us our drinks, she gave me her cell phone. She had called two fellow candidates and friends from her program who had taken the class with her and through this impromptu conference call, they were able to share positive feedback with me on the spot. Later, our waitress told me that the other students were very jealous of her because she'd had the luck to meet me in person. Once again, a face-to-face meeting confirmed for me that my insistence about creating community and transmitting my personal influence were definitely possible in an online setting.

I now regularly teach a split schedule of on-campus and online courses each semester, and it's always interesting to see that we do get to know each other very well no matter if the course is online or face-to-face. The community remains built and the personal influence carries over. It just took my candidates to free me up so we both could benefit in rich, diverse ways by learning from one another.

ROSELA'S STORY — FACE-TO-FACE VS. ONLINE LEARNING: WHICH IS BEST?

As I reflect on my journey toward having the capacity and skills to teach courses online, clearly it has not been a smooth ride. I hope that my story is inspirational and will help other faculty know that they are not alone. Like Kai in chapter 3, I have always valued the relationships that I have developed and built with my students. This outcome has remained constant from the start of my teaching career, beginning as an elementary school teacher some twenty years ago.

It was quite amazing what I learned about my fourth and fifth grade students beyond the classroom setting. By participating in free-throw basketball competitions or a game of checkers at morning recess, eating lunch in the school cafeteria, and even simply engaging in conversation while on yard duty supported my teaching practices. These moments may seem non-essential in determining what occurs in the classroom environment and how it impacts learning, but for me they were incredibly significant. These are only a few examples to illustrate how I gained insight into who my students were, what interested them, and how they learned best.

Taking the time to get to know my elementary school students made a difference in developing curriculum and teaching concepts that were relevant, active, and engaging. I wanted them to be able to connect with the content in meaningful ways. Since then, I have applied this same instructional practice to my teacher candidates at the university level. For example, at the beginning of each semester, I ask candidates to create "identity bags" that include different artifacts, which reflect their identity in multiple ways. These artifacts might relate to their personal, educational, career, cultural, learner, and/or teacher identities. The purpose of this experience is twofold. One, it highlights the personal narrative of each candidate in our community of learners, and two, it serves as a starting point for candidates to begin to connect with the content of the course.

A second example is a place of interest photo journal that candidates create using online tools to embed voiceover narration, pictures, and/or video to tell the story about a place. This learning experience provides an opportunity for candidates to connect with a place that may hold significance in their lives, a place they choose to further explore or have never visited before.

Lastly, I have found that asking candidates to create and draw a self-portrait can be a powerful learning experience. Their self-portrait assignments have some unique features. One side of their face reflects how they perceive themselves and the other side reflects how they think others perceive them. Within the self-portrait, perceptions may be described with pictures and symbols along with visual art elements and adjectives. The results are always noteworthy and provide a great amount of insight into who my candidates believe and perceive they are. These are a few examples of active experiences that I have integrated into my face-to-face courses that allow me to get to know the candidates and support them in connecting with the course content. Therefore, I was convinced that nothing could replace the face-to-face context for learning.

I was not only hesitant, but also resistant to the possibility that delivering instruction fully online would equally and inclusively support the development and building of the community of learners in a manner that I valued. Then, I was approached by our program director and a colleague to recreate an elementary education course traditionally taught in a face-to-face learning environment to one that could be taught face-to-face, in a hybrid manner, or completely online. In addition, the learning experiences for the course would provide the candidates and instructor both synchronous and asynchronous environments to meet or complete assignments.

The design of this course took me out of my comfort zone and was a tall order given my emerging technology abilities. It disrupted how I valued forming professional relationships with my teacher candidates. It also required me to let go of the notion I held that there was no way online learning could provide that same connection with my candidates or have them engage with one another in a manner similar to a face-to-face context. I had to shift my thinking and see this course design as an opportunity for candidates to be able to access this course when they otherwise could not; to provide other instructional faculty the opportunity to teach this course when they otherwise might not; and even more significant, to overcome the resistance of teaching online that I had clung to for many years. I was anxious and uncomfortable being thrust into this new experience.

As the first instructor to pilot the redesigned course, using modules created for an online context in a face-to-face setting was a new experience for me. Each week, I reflected, refined, and returned to the next class feeling more capable and confident in my capacity to effectively use technology to enhance my teaching and the candidates' experiences. It was definitely a challenging semester, but I persevered.

The next year I delivered this course through a hybrid platform. The semester was organized in three ways: the candidates and I met face-to-face at the university, held whole class synchronous sessions via Zoom, and completed asynchronous sessions where no class was held, and instead, time was designated for candidates to independently complete assigned modules.

Throughout the semester I often questioned the effectiveness and organization of the course and if the candidates were actually learning anything. In addition to the multimedia resources, online tools, and technology skills required as an instructor, the multiple ways that I was connecting with candidates through this hybrid format were overwhelming. Planning for the three different delivery formats, keeping track of each candidate's independent and collaborative tasks associated with the modules, and making appropriate adjustments took an extensive amount of time. Furthermore, I still questioned if I was effectively creating a conducive and positive learning environment where collaborative relationships could thrive in this hybrid setting.

At the end of the semester, I walked away from this experience feeling disappointed and dissatisfied with the outcomes. Like many people in education, I hold myself to a very high standard. At the time, I felt I had not provided the optimal learning experience for my candidates. However, many candidates from that semester expressed otherwise, as evidenced by the evaluations they submitted. I realize now that I did my best and the candidates recognized my effort.

The more opportunities that I have embraced to actively participate in online and distance teaching and learning, the less apprehensive I have become. I am able to engage and connect candidates to the content virtually/

online in similar ways as I did in the in-person learning environment. It just takes creativity and envisioning what class sessions, active experiences, and independent and collaborative assignments will look like in the virtual setting.

While my story poses the question of which is best, my answer is that I now understand that they both serve their purposes and can be profound in their own ways. By embracing the opportunity to teach online, I learned valuable lessons. My biggest takeaway: learn by doing. My second biggest takeaway: develop and form professional relationships with candidates so that they can best connect to the concepts they are learning and ultimately apply those concepts to their lives. Like Makana (literally translated as *gift* or *reward*) in chapter 3, I view my learners as gifts. Developing positive relationships with my candidates and creating a community of learners, whether face-to-face or online is possible and will always be held in high regard.

MARK'S STORY — A MODIFIED HYFLEX MODEL FOR OUR COURSES AND OURSELVES

Although I have served many years as a high school social studies teacher and district administrator, I just completed my first year in higher education in a tenure track position. During my first semester, I was responsible for teaching an introduction to education course face-to-face. After a successful fall semester, I was ready to take on some additional course design; however, little did I realize how much course design would result from the COVID-19 pandemic as all courses transitioned to online teaching and learning during the spring.

I was provided many helpful tools and techniques as well as supportive mentoring and recommendations to successfully move my face-to-face courses online. My focus was to communicate with the teacher candidates, comfort them with the transition, and complete the courses in the best way I could. Now was not the time to totally restructure the content and assignments. Fortunately, the semester ended well, and I realized several new discoveries about my teaching and learning to incorporate into future face-to-face and online courses.

In preparation for fall, my second year in higher education, I have been given the elementary social studies methods course as part of my load. This is a course I am passionate about and I believe has not been fully served by the college. Furthermore, it is a core area in which our students underperform on their licensure exams.

In revising this course and preparing for fall, I am choosing to use a modified hyflex model, which allows the instructor to maintain some teacher-student contact, while leveraging online technology successfully. My current plan is to teach two seventy-five-minute face-to-face class sessions per week with half of the candidates attending on Day 1 and the other half of the candidates attending on Day 2. That means I will teach one face-to-face (F2F) lesson two times per week. In order to cover the curriculum, I will teach another lesson online asynchronously.

My goals for the course are to move from a focus on creating art projects, and fun activities with little scope for deeper learning, to a course in which teacher candidates accurately understand and authentically enact the purposes of elementary school social studies. My desire is for them to fully engage in critical thinking and problem solving associated with the teacher education standards and social studies themes as outlined by the National Council for Social Studies (NCSS, 2010; 2018).

My plan is to build on my knowledge and experiences, align the class sessions with the NCSS themes and standards, and facilitate student-centered, inquiry-based, decision-making learning experiences for teacher candidates that allow them to be actively engaged in challenging explorations connecting social studies concepts and practices within the discipline, across the elementary school curriculum, and into the world both locally and globally. In other words, I want to model elementary school social studies in our methods course in ways the candidates can replicate in their own classrooms.

Originally, I anticipated challenges when teaching my revised version of this course. Those included candidates' course expectations as well as limitations in their abilities to draw upon their own elementary school learning experiences, which might not be to the depth planned for in my revised curriculum. Now, the challenges are increased with my need to allocate and balance the F2F and online portions of this course to achieve meaningful and relevant outcomes through high-quality activities and assignments. Plus, I must always keep my candidates' personal situations at the heart of my plans. Frequently my candidates are experiencing issues associated with equity and access as evidenced by computer, equipment, and internet connectivity issues. The requirements for online teaching and learning in this course must match the full range of my teacher candidates' accommodations.

As the fall semester opens and candidates adjust to this modified hyflex model, my goals are to (a) communicate frequently so all portions of the course are clear and comprehensive; (b) reassure supportively, particularly through online availability as we transition from the previous curriculum and delivery model to the revised curriculum and delivery model; and (c) facilitate collaborative learning using online tools as the candidates and I embark on this new adventure together. For me, the key to the success or failure of course delivery in this modified hyflex model will rest on how I build community, both online, and face-to-face.

V. CAROLE'S STORY—WE DID IT! ALL OF MY INTERNS INTERVIEWED ONLINE AND RECEIVED CLASSROOM TEACHING OFFERS

During the 2020 spring semester, I was supervising interns completing Internship II, their culminating requirement in our undergraduate teacher preparation program. Placed in area middle schools, I usually visited them weekly (individually and in small groups), and they submitted assignments online (completed primarily in their classrooms). When the pandemic began and all of us were sent home, the course expectations and outcomes had to be modified immediately. Some expectations were relatively easy to change; other outcomes required much more creativity.

Transitioning to online teaching and learning was challenging for all of us. I was anxious about the technology, and candidates were anxious primarily about graduating.

As the candidates and I reorganized the remaining weeks of Internship II, we communicated through email and WebEx. The candidates shared initial concerns about their units and lessons; however, soon they expressed much more uncertainty related to completing licensing requirements and finding teaching positions. Interviews for classroom teacher openings usually include at least one, sometimes two or more, F2F conversations with the principal(s), teachers, and even the superintendent and at schools they may not have yet visited.

We usually met F2F in small groups to preview the interview process, prepare for questions, and practice professionalism, but because of COVID-19, all procedures needed to be conducted online. Being fairly new to WebEx, all of us explored the functions and became attentive to the presence of professional demeanors, background distractions, and home (family, pet, and electronic) disruptions. Model interviews were integrated into their presentations and contextualized as if the interns were presenting the televised evening news. Our WebEx sessions were filled with new discoveries.

Together we recognized that candidates need to dress professionally from head to toe as they might step away while the camera is on; be ready to enter the online session early; and practice repeatedly in advance so they know where to look, how they appear and sound, and how to interact appropriately.

I provided feedback for their presentations in three specific categories: overall appearance, interview answers, and professional adaptability. The third category was particularly important for their upcoming online interviews. In addition to being able to quickly think of answers to given scenarios, now the interns would be responsible for the intense focus on their presence and control of technology. Practicing on WebEx provided us new and improved ways of preparing their professional adaptability and polishing for their interviews. Moreover, I became better acquainted with each intern in ways that I had not experienced with face-to-face sessions and gained insights to use with my future interns in both face-to-face and online settings. Next semester, I plan to invite at least one of my interns to be a guest speaker to share their spring experiences with the fall interns.

We survived the spring semester and all of the interns were hired. However, as the new fall semester approaches, I need to move my course from a face-to-face to a WebEx format. From the unanticipated move to online teaching and learning, I have learned that educators need to be incredibly flexible, unflappable, and nurturing.

ERIN'S STORY—PROFESSIONAL DEVELOPMENT IN ONLINE TEACHING AND LEARNING FOR K–12 CLASSROOMS AND MEDIA CENTERS

I prepare media specialists at a university and have served as both a classroom teacher and media specialist. I have also worked with several K–12 teachers and media specialists, as well as colleagues throughout the college of education, who sought help with their transitions to online teaching and learning. During the spring of 2020, those who sought help were particularly in need of information about online discussions that fully engaged learners in whole group and small group conversations. I share below how I supported them as my story.

In response to the requests, I collaborated with an adjunct professor teaching in the Instructional Technology online teaching and learning certification program to design a two-hour professional development (PD) workshop, *Building an Online Space for K–12 Learners*. This PD was offered for free, filled immediately, and generated a waiting list. The workshop was organized on two purposes: (a) detailing the Universal Design for Learning (UDL) guidelines (CAST, 2018) to ground thinking and (b) describing specific tips, tools, and techniques for conducting learner discussion online to explore recommendations.

Universal Design for Learning presents a process of planning to ensure that every learner is successful via three components: multiple means of engagement, representation, and action and expression. Engagement sparks affective networks associated with *Why*. Representation stimulates recognition networks associated with *What*. Action and expression ignite strategic networks associated with *How*. Many options for each component are available on the UDL website and were incorporated into the PD.

We recommend conducting learner-centered online discussions to promote intentional and authentic learner interactions. Our session began by establishing norms and expectations related to online teaching and learning experiences. Then we differentiated between two types of statements of integrity: responsible use and acceptable use. Responsible use emphasizes what to do; acceptable use emphasizes what not to do. Too often educators limit their approaches to acceptable use, which communicates peripheries rather than possibilities. A goal of educators is to promote critical thinking and creativity; making responsible use more appropriate for these outcomes.

We also recommend groups or circles, where learners participate by talking in real time rather than boards or forums where learners type responses to a given prompt or replies to other learners, for online discussions. Tools are available through most online platforms to allow for these types of discussion groups. By practicing with these tools and techniques before launching them with their learners, or rehearsing discussion groups with colleagues, teachers and media specialists will benefit and overcome likely obstacles.

We also built upon cooperative learning purposes and procedures (Johnson & Johnson, n.d.), and limited our online groups to five or six learners, allowing each learner time to talk, listen, and contribute. The members of each group were assigned roles/tasks that the teacher/specialist previewed/organized prior to assigning groups. The roles/tasks included:

- Group Director—ensures that the group stays on topic, and each group member is given the same amount of time to talk.
- Word Warrior—records use of the vocabulary related to their topic.
- Concept Connector—records the networking between text to self, text to text, and text to world. (With experience, more than one Concept Connector can be assigned as each learner has individual lived experiences to share.)
- Idea Illustrator—captures a literal or representative picture of the topic.
- Passage Picker—records key statements in the text used for the group discussion.
- Discussion Summarizer—presents a concise synopsis of the discussion relying upon the notes recorded by the Word Warrior, Concept Connector, Idea Illustrator, and Passage Picker.

After the PD workshop, participants submitted feedback. One comment captured our intent:

> Online teaching and learning is not face-to-face instruction delivered online. Effective online teaching and learning requires time, planning, and careful foresight. The instructor must possess expertise in adaptability, technology, and innovation. Most important, the instructor must provide meaningful feedback to each learner as well as ask for, listen to, and act upon student feedback to improve group discussions. Without these qualities, effective online teaching and learning does not reflect a teacher's ability and success with each learner.

SUMMARY

The *Stories from the Field* show how online teaching and learning can be viewed and handled from the perspective of teacher candidates, teachers, field supervisors, and specialists. As all educators know, no "one-size-fits-all" solution exists to tell us how to best structure, deliver, and adapt the courses we teach. We possess the knowledge and skills, the information and insight we can gain from our colleagues and candidates, and our own desire and determination to become better at what we do for and with our learners.

Finally, as you progress along your journey as an online educator, we wish you the best and leave you with this quote from Eleanor Roosevelt: "The purpose of life is to live it, to taste experience to the utmost, to reach out eagerly and without fear for newer and richer experience."

REFLECTION QUESTIONS

1. How do the stories shared resonate with your own experiences?
2. What was your experience transitioning from face-to-face to online teaching and learning?
3. What is your best "Story from the Field" as it relates to learning to teach an online class?
4. What is your best "Story from the Field" as it relates to teaching an online class?
5. What is your best "Story from the Field" as it relates to taking an online class?
6. How might you incorporate ideas shared in the stories into your own online teaching?

REFERENCES

CAST. (2018). *Universal design for learning guidelines version 2.2.* http://udlguidelines.cast.org/.

Johnson, D. W., & Johnson, R. J. (n.d.) *An overview of cooperative learning.* http://www.cooperation.org/what-is-cooperative-learning.

National Council for the Social Studies (2010). *National curriculum standards for social studies: A framework for teaching, learning, and assessment.* NCSS.

National Council for the Social Studies (2018). *National council for the social studies national standards for the preparation of social studies teachers.* NCSS.

Epilogue

Challenges, Choices, Changes, and Cheers

Erin O. Shaw, Monica K. Amyett, and Nancy P. Gallavan

> *You cannot get through a single day without having an impact on the world around you. What you do makes a difference, and you have to decide what kind of difference you want to make.* —Jane Goodall (n.d.)

When members of the ATE Commission on Online Teaching and Learning began writing this book during the 2019 fall semester, approximately 19.9 million students were enrolled in U.S. universities (National Center for Education Statistics [NCES], 2019). At that time, about 16 percent of university students were enrolled in programs available exclusively via online courses, 18 percent of university students were enrolled in at least one online course, and 65 percent of university students were not enrolled in any online courses (Batrujum, 2020; NCES, 2019). Additionally, one-third of the 19.9 million students anticipated taking at least one online course but they did not anticipate taking the majority of their courses online (Lederman, 2019).

In the fall, 2019, nearly 2,000 universities offered teacher preparation programs (Lynch, 2018) with approximately one-third fewer teacher candidates enrolled in those programs since 2010 due to various reasons, including, ironically, the need for online course availability (Parelow, 2019). Moreover, although some online and hybrid teacher preparation programs and courses were offered for both undergraduate and graduate candidates, face-to-face courses were primarily offered in the majority of undergraduate programs.

To accommodate the increasing demands by candidates, faculty, and administrators to offer teacher preparation courses online, more teacher educators were exploring optional approaches. However, no book was available that was written specifically about online teaching and learning for teacher educators focused on their relationships with university students who are teacher candidates and future K–12 classroom teachers responsible for the teaching and learning of K–12 learners.

Consequently, the purposes of our book were threefold: (a) to mentor and strengthen teacher educators who were already engaged in online teaching and learning, (b) to guide and support teacher educators who were relatively new to online teaching and learning, and (c) to spark and reassure teacher educators considering the transition to online teaching and learning. Members of this ATE commission recognized that the time had arrived to research and publish the knowledge, skills, and dispositions associated with effective online teaching and learning specifically for teacher educators.

Then, during the 2020 spring semester, the world experienced the COVID-19 pandemic, prompting universities to send everyone home. Abruptly, whether they wanted to or not, all teacher education students and faculty were engaged in online teaching and learning. Some students and faculty accommodated this rapid relocation rather easily; other students and faculty experienced the sudden shift with more difficulty. Thus, to fulfill the three purposes of this book, this epilogue focuses on the challenges, choices, and changes impacting teacher educators while concomitantly celebrating the successes and satisfaction with cheers experienced both pre-pandemic and during the pandemic.

Reconnecting with the power of presence, personalization, and possibilities described in this book's introduction, we have identified some challenges, choices, and changes associated with online teaching and learning and grouped them into five categories. The recommendations shared in these five categories will help ensure that your motivation and methods are visible in your course presentation and candidate interactions.

FIVE CATEGORIES OF EFFECTIVE ONLINE TEACHING AND LEARNING

The five categories featured in our book's epilogue include:

Campus Online Services/Liaisons/Mentors
University/College/Department/Program/Self Expectations
Technology/Equipment/Accessibility/IT
Communication/Interactions/Differentiation
Time/Strength/Grace

Campus Online Services/Liaisons/Mentors

For several decades, most universities across the United States have gradually opened offices or centers that provide a variety of services, primarily to faculty, to improve instruction. Initially, campus services were attentive to helping faculty develop curriculum aligned with instruction and assessments, construct meaningful interactive in-class learning experiences, and rethink faculty-student communication and connections. Over time, campus services expanded to focus on online teaching and learning to meet the needs and interests of faculty and students exploring this format. Campus services now offer a full range of courses, workshops, and tutorials, specifically for online teaching and learning.

Online course developers may be called liaisons. One such liaison shared that, pre-pandemic, approximately 15 percent of the faculty at her institution used their services. Overall, only 11 percent faculty at her institution taught online courses, a few faculty used the online grading system, and some faculty used no online tools and technology at all. The liaison explained that, historically, the same 15 percent of the faculty usually attended all of the related courses and workshops. During the last three years more faculty, especially new faculty, were beginning to show interest and become involved. The challenge for the campus online service was expanding new opportunities for the 15 percent while encouraging more participation by the 85 percent.

With the arrival of the pandemic, all faculty at this institution were forced to transition to online teaching and learning; many more faculty quickly found the campus online service. Immediately, courses, workshops, and tutorials tailored to the range of needs and interests were scheduled. Experienced faculty were recruited to assist faculty who were novices to online teaching and learning. However, the liaison shared that, as the fall semester approached, not all faculty had adjusted comfortably to online teaching and learning; some faculty continued to teach and communicate with students exclusively through email. And, yes, some faculty have left higher education due to the requirement to pivot to online teaching and learning.

If you are not already acquainted with your campus services related to online teaching and learning, your first step is to contact that office. Schedule a meeting with one or two liaisons; then, like selecting a physician, establish a meaningful relationship with one liaison. Learn your liaison's office hours and contact preferences (email, text, telephone). Your liaison should be available to answer your big, overarching concerns as well as your small, detailed questions. Again, like your physician, you must be open and honest with your liaison in order to fulfill your responsibilities to your program and learners.

Additionally, your liaison must learn about you and your teaching style. Liaisons want you to find success and satisfaction with online teaching and learning. Most likely, the liaison is acquainted with the expectations of your program, department, and college plus the variety of resources available across campus and online. Plus, with your permission, most liaisons will be able to access your online course to assist you in finding and using various functions.

In addition to developing a relationship with a liaison, watch for and attend online teaching and learning courses and workshops. The information you gain from the other participants will be equally valuable as the information you gain from the developers facilitating the learning experience. From these courses and workshops, you will discover other faculty progressing similarly and/or responsible for courses in the same program as you, allowing you to form new partnerships in learning.

In developing new partnerships in learning, you will benefit greatly by collaborating with another teacher educator to serve as your mentor. Ideally, your mentor should be more advanced than you are with online teaching and learning so the mentor can answer your questions quickly and succinctly as well as offer you some tips and techniques to enhance your layout.

You may discover that you want to have several different mentors due to the colleagues' various strengths, styles, schedules, and so forth. Advances (and advantages) associated with online teaching and learning are becoming available rapidly. Now is the time to learn from everyone around you. Keep in mind, your mentors will also learn from you, and soon you will be mentoring your colleagues with your discoveries.

University/College/Department/Program/Self Expectations

The course format for online teaching and learning may be standardized regarding expectations ranging from some expectations to all of the expectations. Some universities want to make the online course appearances easier for all students to navigate by requiring the same basic functions to be placed in the same location on all courses at that university. Likewise, some universities allow (and limit) faculty options regarding the course appearance, the submission system, or the grade book arrangement. Be aware of all expectations before you invest your time and energy into designing your course.

Discuss course formats with colleagues in your college, department, and program. In addition to complying with university expectations, the teacher educators in your college, department, and program may have adopted their own expectations or some acceptable and other unacceptable options. When several teacher educators are responsible for different sections of the same course, using the same or a similar course format allows teacher educators to focus on the substance, again accommodating teacher candidates.

Many different tools are available for teacher candidates to see, hear, view, read, write, and talk as they interact with online teaching and learning. You are strongly encouraged to incorporate different media into your course. However, be aware of overloading your course with too many requirements. Again, talk with other teacher educators interacting with the same teacher candidates to ensure that, as a group, you are offering your candidates a full array of assorted experiences; curriculum mapping is extremely useful.

Although the layout of your course will reflect your teaching style, always consider your course from the perspective of your candidates' learning styles. Be sure to include an introductory module for your candidates to preview the course and become acquainted with the tools and techniques prior to beginning the first academic module. The introductory module should include documents identifying applicable expectations (and/or links to documents) shared within the university, college, department, and/or program. An effective strategy is to require teacher candidates to complete an assessment as part of the introductory module documenting their knowledge regarding the course syllabus, schedule, expectations, layout, to confirm that they are well-acquainted with the course and ready to begin.

As you encounter the constant stream of new challenges, choices, and changes, be aware of your own teaching/learning style and energy levels. Acknowledge the situations and accept your roles and responsibilities; yet establish appropriate perimeters and pleasures to care for yourself. Find ways to express and exchange questions and concerns with colleagues, and ways to balance all the items you are juggling in both your professional and personal life.

Technology/Equipment/Accessibility/IT

Effective online teaching and learning requires a variety of technology and equipment that must be current and compatible with institutional expectations. Guided by your campus online liaisons and your college/department/program leaders and colleagues, you should be able to acquire the needed technology and equipment, especially as technology and equipment must be supported by the university and updated when needed.

Not only must technology and equipment be available in teacher educators' university offices, technology and equipment must be accessible in teacher educators' homes. Various approaches can be used to provide teacher educators with the necessary tools and techniques to have technology and equipment in both locations. Again, the campus online liaison, college/department/program leaders, and colleagues should be contacted when you need guidance and support. Having the proper tools helps to fulfill your obligations and maximize opportunities.

Teacher candidates, especially candidates new to online teaching and learning, may need to acquire appropriate technology and equipment. Faculty are encouraged to collaborate within the college/departments/programs to establish a necessary, uniform list of technology and equipment for their candidates. The identified items on this list must be framed by the candidates' financial abilities and limitations and include resources related to financial assistance.

Similarly, when candidates are asked to attend class sessions on campus as well as class sessions online, candidates must be provided physical spaces where they can use their computers to attend the online class. Not all teacher candidates live on campus; little time may exist between classes. Consequently, teacher educators must provide instructions for candidates prior to the first day of classes with choices when attending a class session face-to-face and when attending a class session online.

Importantly, teacher candidates who live off-campus may share their accommodations with other students (of all ages) as well as their families who are working from home. When all students are attending their class sessions and families are working online, everyone living in the same accommodation will be accessing the same internet source; plus, they all may be listening to other people talking as they, too, participate in the online conversations.

In addition to the campus online liaison and academic leaders, teacher educators and candidates will need assistance from Information Technology (IT). Many universities offer two types of IT: email services available campus wide and computer services available in colleges. The college IT personnel specialize in the tools and techniques relevant to the college programs, faculty, and students.

All teacher educators must become acquainted with their IT personnel. These colleagues are vital for problem solving in ways that supplement all other services. Be attuned to the expertise offered by your various campus and college services. This information will be extremely useful for you and your candidates.

Communication/Interactions/Differentiation

Three areas of online teaching and learning that require your attention include communication, interactions, and differentiation. These three areas are especially essential as teacher educators are both facilitating the instruction and modeling the demonstration of expectations for candidates to incorporate into their future K–12 classrooms. The process of online teaching and learning emphasizes the power of communication evident in the clarity and comprehension of the communication, the organization (including length) of and outcomes required from the communication, and the timing and techniques used to post the communication. All communications must distinguish information items from actions items by adding helpful words such as "Response Required by (specific date)" in the subject line. When actions are required, identify the purpose, steps, resources, submission process, and due date, preferably in separated sentences for quick and easy reading. The clearer your initial communications, the fewer follow-up communications.

You want to interact online with your teacher candidates more often than you would communicate with them during face-to-face class sessions. Interactions may be with the whole class, small groups, and/or individual candidates. Likewise, you need to provide opportunities online for your candidates to interact with one another both formally and informally. For many candidates, online teaching and learning is relatively new and the more positive and practical experiences you can provide them, the more likely the candidates will learn and complete their programs. Try using multiple ways to talk with your candidates through Zoom and other programs as you develop your own repertoire.

As you interact with your candidates, you will realize that each candidate's situation is unique; the candidate and you will benefit by differentiating appropriately. You are not decreasing expectations; you are modifying expectations in ways that, most likely, will increase both candidate learning (individually and as a group/whole class) and your teaching. Find ways to co-construct various ways of expressing and exchanging outcomes so everyone grows.

Time/Strength/Grace

Contrary to popular belief, online teaching and learning does not require more time; it requires a different sense of time. Most teacher educators did not measure the exact amount of time they spent preparing for their first semester in higher education. Similarly, as you transition to or enhance your online teaching and learning encountering constant challenges, choices, and changes, you are dedicating much of your time to preparing for another first semester. The advantages are if you have experience in higher education, you have already mastered many aspects of effective teaching and learning, at your particular institution, and with your teacher candidates. You are building upon prior knowledge and experiences. Yes, the first few semesters may seem to consume a great amount of your time. Your quest is to find ways to set boundaries so you can maintain balance.

Much like posting office hours, communicate with your candidates the times each day that you are and are not available online or by phone. Also communicate the earliest and latest time of each day that you will answer email and accept submissions to the course. One teacher educator asked candidates to insert the word Urgent into the subject line when the email was urgent; the candidates respected this option and rarely used it. Again, differentiation means accommodating our candidates appropriately.

Capitalize upon your strengths related to both teaching and learning. If you have not taken an online course, you are encouraged to enroll in one soon. Quickly, you will discover your greater strengths and your lesser strengths as a learner. These discoveries will advance both your sense of success and your sense of satisfaction. The irony is, as you are preparing your candidates to become teachers, you will grow into a better teacher by becoming a learner. For more information about your strengths, check out CliftonStrengths (Gallup, n.d.); your university may already provide access to their services.

Many teacher educators have adopted the act of allowing grace with their candidates, especially with online teaching and learning. Your candidates have been raised in many different contexts from which candidates have constructed personalized prior knowledge and experiences. Likewise, your candidates live in many different situations that may or may not be similar to other candidates or teacher educators. The past and the present constitute the content and context that candidates bring to their teacher preparation programs and will take into their future classrooms.

Through the act of grace, you are strongly encouraged to know each candidate's past content and present context so you can co-construct outcomes applicable to a meaningful and relevant future. As you facilitate collaboration with other candidates, you are contributing far more effectiveness benefiting K–12 learners than frequently found patterns of teacher preparation. Plus, when you allow grace, especially to accommodate candidates' needs—technology, tools, techniques, time, and so forth, you are modeling the most important outcome.

Teacher educators who are most comfortable and competent frequently allow the act of grace as a viable option in honor of candidates' collective content and context. Quoting Maya Angelou, "Do the best you can until you know better. Then when you know better, do better" (n.d.).

CHEERS

The abrupt transition to online teaching and learning for teacher educators has generated unintended consequences worth celebrating. Teacher educators have become much more attentive to their courses—the purposes, the pedagogy, and the practicality. More time is dedicated directly to teaching and learning; less time is spent on course management items.

Through meticulous preparation and mindful facilitation, teacher candidates are experiencing new and advanced experiences. Being online requires teacher educators and candidates to read, watch, and listen carefully to information shared via a variety of media perhaps not previously used in their face-to-face classes. Teacher educators are sharing that attendance, participation, and equity have increased. Plus, individual and group conversations coupled with discussion entries and chat postings become more authentic, especially when accompanied with synchronous Zoom sessions.

With all parts of the course documented online, teacher educators and candidates can revisit, reinvest, and reflect on the course content and pedagogical processes. When teacher educators reflect, they can easily identify areas that need improvement and modification. When teacher candidates reflect, they can identify areas that they need to reinforce into their repertoire.

MONICA'S INSIGHTS

Capturing the challenges, choices, changes, and cheers associated with online teaching and learning, Monica shares the following insights as a classroom teacher, instructional coach, and aspiring teacher educator working with a K–12 school district and an institution of higher education.

The COVID-19 pandemic has brought unprecedented change within our K–12 education systems. Teachers, students, parents, and administrators have become subject to new policies and practices that have wreaked havoc on a system that was relatively stable for the past century. We all hear much speculation that our K–12 systems may never return to the previous status and, though this unsettling shift has caused stress and strain in our schools, some of the resulting changes might be long overdue and worth serious consideration.

Perhaps the biggest change that has occurred in schools is the abrupt and total abandonment of the school buildings themselves. Since March of 2020, most schooling has occurred via online platforms as students have been required to attend school from home. This change immediately upended all hard-won advancement related to equitable schooling. No longer are all students traveling to physical spaces wherein teachers and resources are provided to everyone.

The lack of publicly provided structures and functions prohibits many students from leaving a home with limited resources and perhaps unhealthy situations. Some homes are not optimal spaces for online learning. Quiet and organized spaces available for learning may not exist. An educated parent, trusted adult, or an adult who speaks the same language as both the student and the teacher may not be available to encourage engagement or answer questions.

For some students with working parents, all work must be completed in the evenings when, unfortunately, their teachers are not online. Many older students have been required to take on full-time work because their parents lost their jobs. For these students, online learning is taking place when they need rest from their work days. Housing may be in danger; food may be limited; and access to the internet may not be available. These deficits and inequities are of great concern to teachers who dedicate their lives to helping students cope with their circumstances.

However, schools and communities have responded to their students' needs. Many school districts have arranged for food to be taken home and have partnered with cellular internet companies to provide free hotspots to students who do not have internet access. Some internet providers offer free internet to homes for limited periods of time. Some neighborhoods have developed collaborative networks of parents to assist in schooling the children. Though COVID-19 has been disastrous for schools, in some ways, the responses may have enriched communities.

Yet the combination of variability in students' home situations and the dedication of teachers' and administrators' compassion and care frequently has ushered in lowered expectations in student learning. As the fall semester began with a sense of newness, families were offered options for either in-person or online learning. Administrators and teachers have responded by setting new expectations and specific guidelines for online learning. Standards for attendance, learning experiences, and student-teacher interactions have been adopted.

Though administrators offer new promises of equitable learning, the dichotomy in instruction cannot deliver this promise. Some teachers will teach only online classes while other teachers will teach only in person. Because of the perceived automation in online instruction, the online teachers may be assigned as many as three times the number of students the in-person teachers are given to teach. Consequently, online teachers may not be able to develop the important student-teacher relationships or offer meaningful feedback. Teaching and learning practices, which are highly social experiences, will be redefined and much meaning-making will be lost.

The current crisis has upended the system and the psyche of the K–12 teacher. Teachers have been required to undergo a sharp learning curve in technology understanding and use. Though many teachers are adept at using technology in their classrooms, the new situation has added complexity to student-teacher interactions and classroom management. With additional layers to collaborative teacher planning and effective student instruction, the original intent of a meaningful learning experience may be lost in the home and school limitations.

With the opening of the fall semester, administrators struggle with the constant changes. Scheduling was already complex; offering in-person and online instructional options have increased the complexities. Moreover, monitoring everyone's health, maintaining safe environments for total well-being, managing frequent communications with all stakeholders, and making preparations to pivot as mandated by district, state, and federal directives intensifies educators' responsibilities.

Educators tend to hold on to some time-honored traditions. Administrators and teachers invest in our fascination with the next big, new thing. Administrators always seem to be on the hunt for some magical solution, making that sought-after, big difference in learning. Too often, a new teaching methodology, teaching assessment plan, or organizational tool must be learned and adopted by everyone in the school. Most years, teachers are able to accept the new initiative but this year due to COVID-19, teachers are exhausted. Sadly, this year's chaos has taken a toll on teachers.

Some buildings are empty, and due to social distancing, spacing is regulated. Schedules are in constant upheaval. Because of illness and fear, custodial workers and office staff are absent. Some teachers are walking off their jobs and leaving their profession. Other teachers are giving up extracurricular duties that have enriched students' lives (and provided needed income) and still other teachers are simply planning their resignation when the current contract year comes to an end. Teacher burnout was already high but COVID-19 has accelerated this unsettling trend.

Many educators demonstrate hope. Not all teachers are upset or leaving. Some teachers are adapting to the new reality and even embracing the new learning. One example of hope is the creation of a virtual classroom presence. Just as most teachers love to create a welcoming physical space for students, many teachers are taking this practice online and creating virtual rooms, complete with a bitmoji to represent themselves. Teachers are creating a virtual presence to replicate their physical presence. This innovation represents a spirit of perseverance that we need in our teachers.

While many educators have lamented the lack of change in our K–12 systems for years; some teachers are applauding the upheaval because they have spent years waiting and hoping for the system to change. Perhaps the COVID-19 upheaval is exactly what we needed to prompt innovation. Our apple cart has been summarily overturned. Instead of picking up the apples, perhaps we should leave the broken cart behind and find a new mode of transportation.

CONCLUSION

As Monica's insights suggest, the ever-evolving contexts impacting teacher educators' transitions to online teaching and learning (3PLearning, 2020), particularly during the pandemic, require flexibility and the willingness to adopt a new model. We suggest the MECCA Model (Gallavan, 2020) defined by the five components of the MECCA Model include Motivation, Engagement, Creativity, Connections, and Achievement.

The MECCA Model offers a means to help everyone experience a sense of acceptance and well-being. The word mecca means a center, hub, or focus of a group, activity, or interest (Merriam-Webster, n.d.). Online teaching and learning in teacher education certainly encapsulates a group of candidates focused on specific objectives and outcomes both like and unlike face-to-face classrooms. Importantly, any transition to online teaching and learning calls for the teacher educator to keep curricular content and pedagogical practices as intact as possible, yet the teacher educator must offer various, viable options to accommodate each candidate's situation.

Motivation is essential for establishing a warm and welcoming sense of place and belonging; inspiring authentic reasons or incentives to attend, participate, and learn; and emphasizing a meaningful purpose for learning. Engagement means being dynamically involved in ways that are comfortable, collaborative, and co-constructive through various avenues of expression and exchange. Curiosity is promoted and provoked through inquiry and imagination. Learner-centered conversations resonate possibilities and probabilities and reveal flaws and failures.

Connections are generated through exploration, discovery, and reflection; individualized connections and personalized connotations should be threaded through every learning experience attributing to the overall course objectives and outcomes. Built on the motivation, engagement, and curiosity, connections lead to achievement. Achievement is monitored and measured through powerful assessments, especially self-assessments and meaningful feedback from peers and teacher educators.

Each component of the MECCA Model applies to the teacher educator while planning, facilitating, analyzing, and modifying course modules and learning experiences. Teacher educators benefit by identifying each of the five components with the teacher candidates, describing the presence and power of each component throughout both the teacher preparation course and in K–12 classrooms, and modeling each component throughout the course. Second, each component of the MECCA Model applies to all teacher candidates as they navigate the online classroom and complete their discussions, activities, and assignments contextualized in K–12 classrooms. Third, teacher candidates should practice teaching and modeling the five components of the MECCA Model when interacting with K–12 learners. As teacher educators continue to experience the challenges, choices, and changes especially associated with online teaching and learning, they are encouraged to adopt thoughts, actions, and beliefs of readiness, receptiveness, and responsiveness (Gallavan & Merritt, 2018) about themselves, their candidates, their colleagues, and their communities.

REFERENCES

3PLearning. (2020). *5 Challenges of online teaching (and how to rise above them)*.https://www.3plearning.com/blog/5-common-pitfalls-distance-teaching-avoid/

Angelou, M. (n.d.). Quotation. https://www.passiton.com/inspirational-quotes/7525-do-the-best-you-can-until-you-know-better-then.

Batrujum, A. (2020, Apr 12). *Online education statistics*. https://educationdata.org/online-education-statistics/.

Gallup. (n.d.). *CliftonStrengths*. https://www.gallup.com/cliftonstrengths/en/252137/home.aspx.

Gallavan, N. P. (2020, July 31–Aug 4). *Enhancing your f2f and online teaching and learning with the MECCA Model.* [Conference session]. Association of Teacher Educators. Online.

Gallavan, N. P., & Merritt, J. P. (2018). Reinforcing MAT course goals during internship experiences via Gallavan's seven essential elements. In N. P. Gallavan & L. G. Putney (eds.), *ATE Yearbook XXVI: Building upon inspirations and aspirations with hope, courage, and strength: Teacher educators' commitment to today's teachers and tomorrow's leaders* (pp. 43–62). Rowman & Littlefield.

Goodall, J. (n.d.). Quotation. https://www.goodreads.com/quotes/511077-you-cannot-get-through-a-single-day-without-having-an.

Lederman, D. (2019, Dec 11). Online enrollments grow, but pace slows. *Inside Higher Ed*. https://www.insidehighered.com/digital-learning/article/2019/12/11/more-students-study-online-rate-growth-slowed-2018.

Lynch, M. (2018, Jan 31). 2018 Top teacher preparation programs in the United States. *Education Week*. https://blogs.edweek.org/edweek/education_futures/2018/01/2018_top_teacher_preparation_programs_in_the_us.html.

Merriam-Webster (n.d.) Mecca. https://www.merriam-webster.com/dictionary/mecca

National Center for Education Statistics [NCES]. (2019.) *Fast facts: Back to school statistics*. https://nces.ed.gov/fastfacts/display.asp?id=372#:~:text=About%2019.9%20million%20students%20will,in%20fall%202019%20.

Parelow, L. (2019, Dec 3). What to make of declining enrollment in teacher education programs. *Center for American Progress*. https://www.americanprogress.org/issues/education-k-12/reports/2019/12/03/477311/ make-declining-enrollment-teacher-preparation-programs/

About the Editors and Contributors

Monica K. Amyett, PhD candidate, is instructional specialist for the Fort Worth, Texas, Independent School District, Career and Technical Education Department, where she assists CTE teachers in their instructional practice. A clinical fellow with ATE and NAPDS and member of ACTE, she published an article in *Techniques*, the ACTE monthly periodical. Monica taught high school science and engineering for seventeen years. Monica received the Teacher of the Year, Performance Award from the Fort Worth Regional Science and Engineering Fair and the Sarah and Earnest Butler Excellence in Science Teaching Award from the Texas Medical Association. Currently, Monica is researching teacher mindset as science and engineering students engage in classroom design problems at Texas Christian University.

Rosela Carmen Balinbin Santos, PhD, is assistant professor and cohort coordinator at the University of Hawai'i at Mānoa, College of Education in the Institute for Teacher Education, Elementary Education Program working with teacher candidates pursuing a BEd. Her academic interests include elementary school social studies, multicultural education, place-based learning, and school and community partnerships. Rosela serves on the College's Tinalak Filipino Advisory Council and Teacher Education Committee for Social Studies. She is a member of ATE, NCSS, and HSTE. Born and raised on the Island of Maui, Rosela, is also an avid outrigger paddler, having competed in races across Hawai'i and internationally.

Glenda L. Black is associate professor at the Schulich School of Education, Nipissing University. She has worked in the Canadian school system for more than twenty years as a teacher, administrator, and teacher educator. She is the recipient of the Chancellor's Award for teaching excellence and another for research achievement. Awarded numerous federal and provincial grants, Glenda has researched and written extensively on teacher education. Her areas of interest are Indigenous education, international teaching, curriculum development, and action research.

Brandon M. Butler, PhD, is associate professor of social studies education at Old Dominion University in Norfolk, Virginia. He teaches undergraduate elementary school social studies methods and graduate courses in practitioner inquiry, teacher leadership, teacher education, and curriculum and instruction. These courses are offered in face-to-face, hybrid, and asynchronous online formats, and he has led the development of several online programs and individual online courses. He has published extensively on the topics of teacher educator development, self-study research, and social studies teacher education. This research has been published in books and journals including *Teaching and Teacher Education*, *Studying Teacher Education*, *Action in Teacher Education*, *Theory and Research in Social Education*, and *Social Education*.

Marie Byrd is associate professor and director of the College of Education at the University of South Florida Sarasota–Manatee campus. Her public school background is in urban education with years of service in Miami, Florida, as teacher and administrator. Byrd serves on the board of directors of ATE and SRATE and is past president of FATE and SRATE. Her research directs attention to the need for a paradigm shift to engage teachers and leaders in professional development centered on culturally responsive instruction to meet the needs of today's diverse student population.

Mark M. Diacopoulos, PhD, is assistant professor in the Department of Teaching and Leadership, at Pittsburg State University, Kansas. Mark has been as educator for over twenty-five years. He currently teaches courses in social studies methods, curriculum and assessment, explorations in education, and instructional technology as well as supervising interns and student teachers. Mark writes about teacher supervision; identity transitions from student to teacher, and teacher to teacher-educator; instructional technology, including mobile learning in social studies and online learning. He's also a soccer fan, retired martial artist, podcaster, and parent, not necessarily in that order.

Rayna R. H. Fujii, PhD, is assistant specialist and the Elementary Statewide Coordinator at the University of Hawai'i Mānoa College of Education, Institute for Teacher Education, Elementary Education Program. She specializes in elementary social studies, introduction to multicultural education, introduction to teaching, field supervision, and hybrid learning models for the statewide program. Her research interests include elementary school social studies education, social studies for social justice, and online/distance learning education for teacher preparation. Fujii has presented at numerous conferences with organizations such as ATE, AERA, NCSS, SOTF, TCC, IICE Hawai'i, ACEID, and the Kevin Kumashiro Social Justice Conference.

Lori Fulton, PhD, is associate professor of teacher education at the University of Hawai'i at Mānoa in the Institute for Teacher Education, Elementary Education Program. She specializes in elementary science education and elementary teacher preparation. Her research interests include the oral and written discourse of science, teacher preparation and professional development, PDS/University partnerships, and place-based pedagogy. She is active in ATE, ASTE, NSTA, and NAPDS.

Nancy P. Gallavan, PhD, is professor emerita of teacher education at the University of Central Arkansas in the Department of Teaching and Learning where she specialized in classroom assessments, cultural diversity and inclusion, doctoral studies, field supervision, and instructional coaching with more than 200 peer-reviewed publications. Active in AERA, ATE, KDP, SRATE, and ArATE, Nancy has received awards for her teaching, scholarship, service, dedication to cultural diversity and inclusion, and student sponsorship at the university and college highlighted by the ATE Distinguished Member Award, ATE Distinguished Mentoring Award, SRATE Distinguished Member Award, and KDP Honorary Eleanor Roosevelt Chapter Legacy Award.

John K. Hicks, PhD, is assistant professor in the Secondary Education and Foundations of Education Department at Slippery Rock University of Pennsylvania where he specializes in English language arts education, teaching of the humanities, accommodating English learners, and the history and philosophy of education. Active in ATE and PAC-TE, John has been nominated for SRU's Teacher Excellence Award each year for the past eight years and has been nominated for SRU's Academic Advising Award three times in the past five academic years.

Ashlie R. Jack, PhD, is assistant dean/accreditation officer and associate professor at Wichita State University in the College of Applied Studies. Jack specializes in accreditation, program assessment, educator preparation, academic vocabulary, and content literacy instruction. She has multiple presentations and publications on each of these areas of research at the regional, national, and international level. Jack is actively involved in the Association of Teacher Educators (ATE) at both the national and state level.

Shirley Lefever, PhD, is dean of the College of Applied Studies (formerly College of Education) at Wichita State University. She has served in this role since 2015. Lefever's previous experiences in higher education include fourteen years at the University of Arkansas where she was involved in developing and delivering teacher preparation programs steeped in clinical practice based on a professional development school model and received the Outstanding Teaching Award for the College of Education. Additional recognitions of her service and leadership include being a recipient of the ATE Distinguished Member Award, the Women Who Lead Award from the Wichita Business Journal and the President's Innovation and Phenomenal Woman of the Year awards from Wichita State University.

Winnifred (Winnie) Namatovu, PhD, is assistant professor of middle grades and secondary education at the University of North Georgia in the Department of Middle, Secondary, and Science Education. Her teaching and research interests are diversity and inclusive pedagogy, social justice education, middle and secondary education, and math education. She is a member of ATE, AMLE, KDPi, NAME, and NCTM.

Walter S. Polka, EdD, is professor of Leadership at Niagara University and coordinator of the PhD Program in Leadership and Policy. He has chaired over fifty doctoral dissertations at three different universities: Georgia Southern University, Niagara University, and Addis Ababa University, Ethiopia. He was a high school social studies teacher, K–12 curriculum coordinator, assistant superintendent for curriculum and instruction, and superintendent of schools in New York. Polka has received several honors and awards during his career and is most proud of receiving the 2013 *Distinguished Alumni Award* from the State University of New York at Buffalo Graduate School of Education.

LeAnn G. Putney is professor in educational psychology at the University of Nevada, Las Vegas. She earned her PhD with emphasis in language, culture, and literacy from the University of California, Santa Barbara. LeAnn specializes in teaching various courses in qualitative research. Her ethnographic research has focused on how teachers and students construct collective classroom efficacy from a Vygotskian perspective, illustrating how efficacy is developed and enhanced. LeAnn has been involved in ATE, NVATE, AERA, TESOL, EQRC, and CARE organizations. She has received awards in teaching, research, collaborative work, and service, and has co-founded a charter school for underserved populations.

Amanda M. Rudolph is professor of secondary education at Stephen F. Austin State University. She teaches in both the undergraduate and graduate programs. She earned her PhD from the University of Arkansas in Curriculum and Instruction with an emphasis in arts education and has published two books, one on classroom management and one on education reform. Rudolph has also served on the board of directors for the Association of Teacher Educators, the Texas Association of Teacher Educators, and the Consortium of State Organizations for Texas Teacher Education and is serving as president and chair for the latter two. Currently, Rudolph is researching gifted and talented education and acting as Vice Chair of the Parent Resource Committee for the Texas Association of Gifted and Talented. She served as editor or co-editor for Teaching Education and Practice, TxEP: Texas Educator Preparation, and the Texas Forum of Teacher Education.

Erin C. Shaw, EdD, NBCT, is assistant professor at the University of Central Arkansas in the Department of Leadership Studies where she specializes in K–12 School Library instruction, online teaching and learning, digital citizenship and instructional technology. Currently, she is the Graduate Program Coordinator for both the Library Media and Information Technologies program and the Instructional Technology program. Active in AAIM, ALA, and AASL, Erin was named the Arkansas Association of Instructional Media (AAIM) School Librarian of the Year in 2014 and received the AAIM Pat McDonald Individual Achievement Award in 2016.

V. Carole Smith, PhD, is professor at Arkansas Tech University, in the Department of Curriculum and Instructions where she specializes in middle grades education. V. Carole has thirty years of public school experience, with twenty of those years as a school and central office administrator. V. Carole has been active in ATE through numerous presentations and various committees. She is former state president of ArATE and has been active with the Association of Middle Level Education through presentations and work with the middle level SIGS.

Amy Earls Thompson, PhD, is assistant professor of reading at the University of Central Arkansas in the Department of Elementary, Literacy, and Special Education where she also serves as program director of the MSE in Reading and Dyslexia endorsement. She specializes in assessment and intervention with students with dyslexia and other reading difficulties, using technology with struggling learners, and field supervision, Amy is dedicated to teaching, scholarship, and service in the field of reading and dyslexia. Amy is a National Board Certified Teacher in Literacy and is active in ATE, ArATE, ILA, ALA, and IDA.

Jon Yoshioka, PhD, is professor and department chair of the Master of Education in Teaching program at the University of Hawai'i at Mānoa's

Institute for Teacher Education. His research interests include teacher education, teacher preparation and professional development, transnational education, PDS/University partnerships, and culturally responsive pedagogy. Jon taught in both public and private schools and is part of the ongoing collaboration that created the first complex-wide Professional Development School (PDS) partnership between the University of Hawai'i at Mānoa College of Education and a complex (five elementary schools, one intermediate school, one high school) of Hawaii Department of Education schools.

Made in the USA
Columbia, SC
27 May 2025